Return to Havana

The Decline of Cuban Society under Castro

Return

to **H**avana

The Decline
of Cuban Society
under Castro

by
Maurice Halperin

VANDERBILT UNIVERSITY PRESS
Nashville ■ *1994*

First Edition 1994
94 95 96 97 98 99   5 4 3 2 1

This publication is made from recycled paper and meets the minimum requirements of
American National Standard for Information Sciences--Permanence of Paper for Printed
Library Materials ⊗

Library of Congress Cataloging-in-Publication Data
Halperin, Maurice, 1906-
Return to Havana: the decline of Cuban society under Castro / by Maurice Halperin
p.   cm.
Includes bibliographical references and index. ISBN 0-8265-1250-X
1. Cuba--Economic conditions--1959-   2. Cuba--Social conditions--1959-
I. Title.
HC152.5.H35 1994
306' .097291--dc20   91-41059
                                    CIP

Manufactured in the United States of America

To the Memory of

Edith

Contents

Acknowledgments

I am grateful to Dr. William Saywell, former president of Simon Fraser University, for funding and otherwise facilitating my trip to Cuba. I have benefited from the flow of newspaper clippings provided by Arnold Court (*Los Angeles Times*), Judith and Hillel Gamoran (*Chicago Tribune*), David Halperin (the Mexican press), and Theodore Halperin (*Boston Globe*). Judith Gamoran and David Halperin read parts of the manuscript and made valuable suggestions. Antonio Cabal Rodríguez, a Cuban graduate student at Simon Fraser University, was helpful in many ways. Bard Young provided skilled and imaginative editorial guidance in shaping the manuscript.

Portions of the text have appeared or will appear in the journals *Society: Social Science and Modern Society* and *Cuban Studies* as well as in *Cuban Communism*, Eighth Edition, edited by Irving L. Horowitz.

Return to Havana

*The Decline of Cuban Society
under Castro*

1 ★ *Introduction*

MY INTEREST IN CUBA GOES BACK to 1935 when I was invited by Waldo Frank, chairman of the now long extinct League of American Writers, to join the playwright Clifford Odets as part of a "civic" committee put together to go to Cuba. The purpose was to investigate—and confirm—reports of horrendous abuse of striking workers by General Fulgencio Batista's dictatorship, the same Batista overthrown by Fidel Castro twenty-four years later. I was not a member of the League, like Odets, but apparently Frank was having trouble recruiting his quota for the committee. When I accepted the invitation—I was then teaching at the University of Oklahoma, in Norman, and had published several articles on Latin American topics—I did not know the project was organized and probably funded by the American Communist party. But that is another story.

The trip began in New York with a rousing public send-off. Eminent sponsors like Archibald MacLeish and Carle-

ton Beals made stirring speeches. However, when the steamer landed in Havana, we were taken into custody on the
dock and transferred by armed police launch across the harbor to the immigration detention center in Tiscornia. Twenty-four hours later we were placed aboard the same steamer
that had brought us to Cuba, and we promptly headed back
to New York. Before we left Tiscornia, Odets received a
cable expressing undying solidarity from his intimate friend
and renowned stage actress Tallullah Bankhead. It was
addressed to "Pisscornia, Havana, Cuba," which injected
some humor into an otherwise melancholy episode. When I
met Che Guevara in Moscow in 1960 and told him that
story, he declared that I could claim to be a precursor of the
Cuban Revolution, and he invited me and my wife, Edith,
to visit Cuba. "This time," he said, "I promise you will not
be deported."

Ernesto Guevara, better known as "Che," was already a
legendary figure when I met him. A foot-loose Argentine
physician, he was recruited by Fidel Castro in Mexico,
where the future guerrillas were in training prior to invading
the island in early December 1956. Che was the only non-
Cuban in Castro's band, chosen primarily because he was a
doctor.

Nevertheless, he turned out to be Castro's best field
commander, eventually writing a text on guerrilla warfare
that gained international recognition. Early on, Che, an
independent Marxist, established the reputation of an

uncompromising enemy of imperialism, at the same time favoring Chinese-style socialism over the Soviet brand. In Cuba, and among his admirers in many countries, Che came to embody the spirit of revolutionary self-sacrifice and the highest idealism.

Che was probably the only true intellectual in Cuba's revolutionary leadership, including Fidel. He had benefited from a broad classical education in Buenos Aires, in addition to his medical studies. He wrote poetry, and his prose works had merit. As a personality, Che was an impressive figure, in part because of his expressive facial features, in part because of his intellect. In spite of his unswerving devotion to Marxist ideals, Che was known to be fair-minded toward Cubans critical of the Castro regime, unlike Fidel, who was vindictive. In the eyes of his leftist admirers worldwide, the defeat of his guerrilla band and his capture and execution in the Bolivian jungles in 1967 moved him from the status of revolutionary hero to that of revolutionary martyr.

It is not at all likely that I would have become involved in the Cuban Revolution if it had not been for my chance encounter with Che Guevara in Moscow. At the same time, my presence in Moscow was itself the product of a long series of remarkable accidents and largely unplanned events. How I got there speaks in miniature of the huge events of the century.

I was born in Boston, Massachusetts, in 1906. My parents were freethinking Jews who had emigrated from czarist Ukraine. I learned from them about the pogroms in the old country and also something about the writers they admired, Ralph Waldo Emerson, Walt Whitman, and the great seventeenth-century heretic, Baruch Spinoza. At the venerable Boston Public Latin School, where I enrolled in 1919, I received a solid grounding in Latin, Greek, and French and in ancient Greek and Roman history. All of those elements initially shaped my understanding of the human condition.

My adult comprehension of the world developed when I was a student at Harvard. As an undergraduate in the mid-1920s, I concentrated in the Romance languages and literatures, principally French. My immersion in French letters and history left a lasting impression on me. The skepticism of Montaigne, the ribald humanism of Rabelais, the critical discourse of Voltaire, Rousseau, and Diderot, the ideals of the French Revolution—*liberté, égalité, fraternité*—these became my models of intellectual probity and social justice. In a strange, unpredictable manner they created the nonconformism that contributed to the great personal crisis that many years later took me to Moscow, then to Havana, and finally back to North America.

In 1931, with the help of an American Field Service Fellowship, I completed my doctorate in comparative literature at the Sorbonne. Also, I had the good luck of being appointed an instructor in the faculty of letters, where I gave a course in the program on North American literature and civilization headed by the eminent professor Charles Cestre. As I look back, the years spent in Paris added to my earlier Francophilia at Harvard and played a decisive role in my intellectual development. Paris was for me what it is for so many, an inexhaustible treasure of historical monuments and a repository of great works of art. It was also a model of sophisticated political debate and civilized living—at the time, a center of American and other expatriate literary and artistic creation. In addition, I found the high academic standards at the Sorbonne and related institutes at the University of Paris and the adjacent Collège de France to be impressive, even though I had been educated at one of the foremost American universities.

In September 1931, having returned to the States, I began the first in a stretch of ten years as an assistant, and then associate, professor of modern languages at the University of Oklahoma. It was during the depths of the Great Depression, when finding a university teaching job was nearly miraculous. At the time, Norman, Oklahoma, was something of an oasis in a cultural desert, although still bound by southern Jim Crow conventions. Thousands of impoverished and dispossessed farmers, the famous Okies of Steinbeck's *Grapes of Wrath*, passed through Norman as they moved west toward California. Their plight moved me and convinced me of the need for deep political and economic reform. So did the dust storms that my colleague Paul Sears described in *Deserts on the March*, his pioneer book on ecological disaster. However, local politicians and other members of the establishment offered no remedy. State politics pitted rabble-rousing demagogues against reactionary oil corporations, and the influence of the once powerful Ku Klux Klan still had to be reckoned with. Franklin Roosevelt's New Deal seemed to be happening in another country.

If Norman could be described as an oasis of enlightenment, it was a besieged oasis. The bulk of the faculty was prudently silent on public affairs. A few voiced sympathy for Mussolini and Hitler but at no risk from the prevailing conservative public opinion. Several others, I among them, took up the cudgels for the old-fashioned American virtues of the Bill of Rights, fair play, the welfare of the underdog, and the New Deal. We were hounded by the big press and investigated for subversion by the Oklahoma state senate, but no Communists were found. Nevertheless, several professors were severely reprimanded and, in my case, a recommendation was handed down that I be fired from the university. The Board of Regents complied, and in July 1941, I was dismissed without any sort of bill of particulars. The only reason given was that it was "for the good of the university." Later, under a new university president, I was reinstated and given a paid predated sabbatical leave of absence on the understanding that I would never return.

I did not consider myself a ring leader of our radical group, but the state senate, influenced by the Ku Klux Klan, apparently considered the only Jewish member something of a kingpin. If I was less than a subversive mastermind, I was clearly imprudent. With a wife and two small children and a mortgaged house, I gave less attention to keeping my job than "doing the right thing." I had been conditioned by my parents and the ideals of the French Renaissance of the sixteenth century and the Enlightenment of the eighteenth—along, no doubt, with some quirk of biochemistry. I remember during the dark days in Norman encouraging Edith not to worry. "Look, if we lose the battle in Oklahoma," I playfully reassured her, "we can always return to the United States." Little did we realize that the events in Oklahoma were a preview of the major political calamity that was to overtake the United States shortly after the end of the Second World War, the period we now call the McCarthy era.

Losing my job in Oklahoma was one step leading to my adventure in Cuba twenty years later. The Oklahoma experience was significant for another reason. I became a close friend of two Latin American colleagues in the modern language department. In addition, Mexico was not far away and naturally attracted my attention. Gradually my publication and teaching activities began to focus on Latin American civilization and the Spanish language. Without my planning it, that shift in my academic focus was essential preparation for a new job in Washington and my eventual journey to Cuba.

The likelihood of American participation in World War

II rescued me from unemployment. In October 1941, I was invited by Preston James, our leading Latin American geographer, to join what was soon to become the Office of Strategic Services (OSS), headed by General William Donovan, the Wall Street lawyer who was an infantry colonel in World War I and had won the Medal of Honor, earning him the sobriquet Wild Bill Donovan. I spent nearly five years in Washington, during the last three as chief of the Latin America Division, in the Research and Analysis Branch headed by William Langer, the distinguished Harvard historian. It was an exceptional learning experience. It meant participating in and frequently directing complex research projects with seasoned, variously trained scholars: economists, anthropologists, political scientists, historians, geographers, and military specialists among others. In my own Latin America Division, I had the support of such top-ranking scholars as historian Woodrow Borah, political scientist Karl Deutsch, and anthropologist Alexander Lesser. For me, it was an intensive postdoctoral education in the social sciences that converted me from a mainly literary scholar to a political specialist and pioneer in interdisciplinary area studies. It turned out to be an indispensable preparation for my later concern with Fidel Castro's revolution.

My association with the OSS became a decisive experience in another sense. It resulted in my becoming a target of the great postwar U.S. Senate inquisition aimed at exposing the infiltration of subversives in the State Department, OSS, and other government agencies during the Roosevelt administration. My record in Oklahoma, followed by indiscretions in Washington, drew the attention of the "Red hunters." I had submitted highly critical reports of the State Department, and particularly the FBI, for biased treatment of our wartime leftist allies in Latin America. I compounded the indiscretion by pursuing personal contacts with American and foreign Communists.

In March 1953, I was brought before the Communist-hunting committee of Indiana Senator William Jenner. Under oath I denied the charge of espionage for the Soviet Union, or any other country, but I refused to answer all other questions ("Are you now or have you ever been a member of the Communist party?"), relying on the protection of the Fifth Amendment of the U.S. Constitution concerning self-incrimination. As Lillian Hellman once put it, it was "scoundrel time." Hundreds of former government officials were being pursued. Alger Hiss was unsuccessfully fighting to stay out of jail. The Rosenbergs were facing execution. Along with reasons of principle concerning my constitutional rights, I was aware of the risk of exposing myself and others ("Do you know so-and-so?") in the hostile environment of the inquisition.

However, there was a price to be paid for "taking the fifth," as it was called by most of the press. Since 1949 I had been head of the Department of Regional Latin American Studies at Boston University. I had been creating an innovative interdisciplinary area studies program, with some success. Our research on the São Paulo region in Brazil, and my general promotion of Brazilian studies, led to my being decorated by the Brazilian government with the Order of the Southern Cross. One of my graduate students, Virgilio Barco Vargas, eventually became president of Colombia. My conduct before the Jenner committee led to a protracted and disagreeable ordeal of questioning by Boston University, under strong outside pressure and with a frightened faculty and passive student body. The result was at first suspension and then dismissal. Thus in late 1953, Edith and I drove to Mexico City to begin a new chapter in our lives.

Mexico was not exactly terra incognita. We had spent a good deal of time there during the 1930s. I had written extensively and sympathetically of the Cárdenas reforms and had developed friendly personal relations with some of the leading political figures of the time. My encounter with the U.S. Senate and subsequent dismissal from Boston University had been reported in the Mexican press, which enhanced my reputation in Mexico's still dominantly anti-Yankee political and intellectual circles. In no time at all, I was doing work for several government agencies, including the National Bank of Mexico, while lecturing at the National University. Edith, an experienced teacher, was almost immediately employed by the American School.

Our combined income provided the wherewithal for renting an ample modern apartment in a pleasant part of the city so that we generally enjoyed a comfortable life. It was not paradise, however. We had no job security, and I had little time for my personal research interests, although the university did publish *La América Latina en transición*, a short book containing a series of my lectures. Most troublesome were my health problems related to recurring gastric disorders. During our fourth year we began to think about leaving. But to where? I was blacklisted in the United States and did not relish peddling encyclopedias as a way to make a living. I wrote to an old friend in Ontario about finding a university job in Canada. After canvassing the possibilities, he wrote back, "While we are not firing our own subversives, we are not taking on foreign subversives."

At that point, my appetite for adventure took over. Why not take advantage of my peculiar situation and try to find a job in the Soviet Union? There would be nothing to lose. I had no pension to protect, and I had already been labeled a Communist and Soviet spy. On the one hand, it would be the experience of a lifetime. The Khrushchev thaw was under way, and the crimes of Stalin had been exposed. What was really going on in the enigmatic world of Marxism-Leninism? On the other hand, what were the possibilities of finding a job in that tightly controlled system?

I discussed the matter with two good friends: Narciso Bassols, one-time member of Cárdenas's cabinet and former Mexican ambassador to the USSR; and Lombardo Toledano, a leading intellectual in the Cárdenas entourage and founder of the Confederation of Mexican Labor. They agreed to sponsor my admission as a visiting scholar. We reached Moscow at the end of 1958. Shortly thereafter, I had a job as senior visiting research fellow at the Institute of the World Economy and International Affairs in the Academy of Sciences of the USSR.

It was, indeed, the experience of a lifetime. Eventually, however, the bureaucratic constraints and intellectual suffocation became unbearable. Again the question, where next? One alternative was to return to the United States, where the teaching blacklist was beginning to be relaxed. The other was to embark on another bold adventure by taking up Che Guevara's earlier invitation. That we were able to do through the Cuban embassy. Thus, Edith and I appeared in Havana in the late summer of 1962, on the eve of the nuclear missile crisis. I had been fortified by my Latin American expertise, my OSS experience, and an intimate exposure to the Soviet system, altogether a useful preparation for delving into the mysteries of the Cuban Revolution.

EDITH AND I remained in Cuba for six years. During that time I taught economic geography at the University of Havana and served as advisor to Marcelo Fernández, Castro's minister of foreign trade. I knew little about foreign trade, but I was helpful, like the proverbial one-eyed person in the land of the blind. Meanwhile, Edith taught English in a foreign language school maintained by the ministry for its employees.

In the spring of 1968, we moved to Vancouver, British Columbia, where I joined the faculty at the newly established Simon Fraser University, and where I still remain. Ever since, I have annually given a course on the Cuban Revolution. My first book on Cuba was published in 1972 and the second in 1981.* In the summer of 1988, I gave my course on the Cuban Revolution at Harvard University and became a consultant to the Nuclear Crisis Project then under way at Harvard's Center for Science and International Affairs.

For some time I had felt the need to return to Cuba to get firsthand impressions of an aging and, in some respects, failing revolution and to renew contacts with those friends I could still locate. To my very great misfortune, Edith, my cherished and inseparable companion of sixty years, died before we could make the trip together. Consequently, I went to Havana alone, arriving on November 5, 1989, and departing the following December 5. Had she been with me, her observations on Cuba "then and now" would have greatly enriched this book.

My first impressions of Cuba "now" actually came before reaching Havana. Anticipating possible delay in obtaining a visa, I applied to the Cuban consulate in Toronto six months before my intended date of departure. An

---

* *The Rise and Decline of Fidel Castro: An Essay in Contemporary History* and *The Taming of Fidel Castro* (both Berkeley: University of California Press).

application form reached me three months later, and the visa itself arrived just a few days before I was to leave. The whole process was a painful ordeal, clearly due to bureaucratic arrogance, sloth, and incompetence. I was uncomfortable and felt insecure on the six-hour flight from Toronto. The Soviet jet used by Cubana de Aviación appeared to be an ancient model. The exterior needed a coat of paint, the interior a complete refurbishing. The toilets were of the no-flush variety. The stewards and stewardesses were lackadaisical and moved slowly. Aggravating my discomfort were my suspicions about the hygienic standards in the handling of food and refreshments.

After the long and wearing flight, we landed in Cuba at Varadero Beach, where most of the passengers, who were Canadian tourists, got off. It was already dark. The rest of us waited and stretched our legs for about a half hour before flying on to Havana. We looked around. The airport was brand-new. The terminal building was modest but spic-and-span, in contrast to the plane. The scene was reassuring. Then I noted two misspelled signs over the wide sliding glass doors leading to the tarmac—GATTE I, GATTE II— a small but significant indicator of "socialist" failure. Perhaps a half-million people in Cuba are completely fluent in English. It should have been easy to get the spelling correct in a brand-new terminal built to promote tourism, designated by Fidel Castro to be a priority industry because of Cuba's desperate need for hard currency. I wondered about other blunders that I had no time to notice as I boarded the plane for the short flight to Havana.

It was about eight o'clock in the warm and humid evening when we reached José Martí International Airport. As far as I could tell, it had not changed in a quarter century. It was overflowing with traffic, which had multiplied several fold since my leaving in 1968. In a dimly lighted shed with no toilet facilities, long lines of newly arrived passengers, mostly from Eastern Europe, inched past immigration checkpoints and, in the next shed, toward customs inspection. Mercifully, the sheds were air-conditioned. Once outside, a crush of hundreds—it seemed like thousands—of people waited for debarking passengers. It was dark, noisy, and overly warm and humid as I tried to locate a University of Havana official who was supposed to meet me. After an hour I gave up. I made my way with my loaded baggage cart to a tiny official tourist office on the grounds and dropped exhausted into the only armchair. A kindly buxom woman listened to my story. She phoned the university, but it was Sunday night: no answer. The big problem was the hotel. I had no reservation. After much phoning, she reported there was not a single vacancy in all of Havana that night.

I stumbled out of the office dragging my baggage cart. By that time, close to eleven o'clock, I had been on the road nearly seventeen hours. The crowd had thinned out and so had the taxis, but one of the specially marked tourist cabs (which accepted only U.S. dollars) was available. A half hour or so later we pulled up to the familiar Habana Libre in the center of town. A porter appeared and, no doubt believing I had a reservation, transferred my bags to his cart and led me to the registration counter. The reply was not unexpected: "Sorry, we don't have a single vacant room." I had prepared my answer: "Compañera, I'm an octogenarian, I've been traveling since early morning, and I'm dead tired. I'll just lie down here on the floor. I hope you won't mind if I take my shoes off." Two or three clerks huddled together, then one went back to an inner office. In a few moments she returned and announced I could have a room. Whether it was because of my salutation ("*compañera*" means "comrade") or my threat to remove my shoes or simply compassion for an *ochentón*, I was given a room on the eighteenth floor, where I remained until leaving for Miami on an American plane, precisely one month later.

Altogether, it was not the most auspicious beginning to my new Cuban adventure. As it turned out, the nature of my arrival was a forecast of much that lay ahead.

2 ★ *Two Cities*

BEFORE MOVING TO HAVANA, WE HAD lived for nearly three years in Moscow. For the Western foreign resident, Moscow in the early 1960s was by and large a cheerless city, physically and intellectually. Our living quarters, in a brand-new but shoddy apartment building, were poorly finished, cramped, and supplied with primitive appliances. The cage-style self-service elevator moved at a snail's pace. From our bedroom window we looked down on an ancient rural scene: several dozen log cabins set along winding lanes (muddy in springtime), with a couple of communal outhouses. We could see people lined up on a winter morning with the temperature at forty below zero. It was one of the last of the hundreds of villages that until then existed side by side with urban Moscow. Before we left for Cuba, the settlement below us was demolished and the inhabitants were scattered among new urban-style dwellings like ours. On the morning the demolition began, we went down to observe the commotion more closely. Elderly women were weeping not with joy but with sorrow at the separation from friends and neighbors, at the loss of community.

The larger city was only occasionally more attractive and convivial. The front of our building faced the Hotel Ukraine, a hideous monster of pretentious grandeur and wasteful use of space, a classic of Stalinesque gothic. In the cavernous lobby, a coffee bar served a tepid, brown, flavorless beverage. The newsstand carried two English-language publications: the then thoroughly orthodox weekly *Moscow News* and the somewhat less dull London *Daily Worker*. After going through endless red tape, I was finally allowed to subscribe to the *New York Times*, a concession to a foreigner. Although it was the period of the Khrushchev thaw, glasnost was still in the distant future. Foreigners were tolerated but not trusted. We always assumed our flat was bugged. It was difficult to hold a candid conversation with a Muscovite and impossible to exchange house visits, except with former gulag inmates. They had been released by Khrushchev and felt they were immune from further punishment. From them we got firsthand reports of the horrors of the Stalin era.

Diversions were few and not readily available. Russian movies were usually dreadful potboilers or dull propaganda. I even had a bit part in one of them in 1961. I forget the title, but it dealt with a famous academik, a prerevolutionary specialist in livestock breeding. The specialist is persuaded by Lenin to work for the newly established Communist regime. In one incident in the film, he goes to the United States to buy high-grade breeding sheep. I was invited by Mosfilm, the giant Soviet film monopoly, to play the role of an American professor whose job was to try to swindle the Russian. My character tries but, needless to say, fails. The academik is far too wise to be fooled or corrupted by a greedy American.

More than the actual filmmaking, I remember the setting for the cinematic exposé. We were on location for a week on the steppes, about fifteen hundred miles southeast of Moscow. It was supposed to simulate the prairies of Kansas. The town in which Edith and I were quartered (I have forgotten its name) was in a deplorable state of disrepair, with muddy streets and mainly empty stores. A large brick communal outhouse dominated one of the main squares. The stench was unbearable. A large red banner over the entrance bore the customary legend: "Hail to Our Glorious Communist Party."

Back in Moscow, concert and ballet tickets were hard to come by. So we did a lot of walking, weather permitting, and sightseeing on foot. The Kremlin was a jewel; Arbat Street and the GUM shopping galleries had a quaint nineteenth-century flavor; Gorki Park in summer was pleasant. But most of Moscow was unattractive, and people seemed to reflect the city's grayness. They wore stained and ill-fitting clothes and rarely smiled. "It's a short-sleeved, stern-faced city," said our friend Albert Maltz one day as we pushed our way through a crowd coming out of the subway, "reminds me of Scranton, Pennsylvania."

In great contrast for someone coming from Moscow, Havana was an astonishing city in the summer of 1962. My first impression was that of a cosmopolitan "first world" capital. The streets were lined with graceful, colorful facades, suffused with tropical light and teeming with neatly dressed, gesticulating people. Despite the heat, the absence of body odors, even in the crowded buses, was remarkable. Obviously, unlike Muscovites, *Habaneros* bathed and changed clothes frequently and used deodorants. Something that struck us soon after arriving was the absence of drunks in the streets or sprawled out in doorways, a common sight in Moscow. Once, a few years later, during an early evening walk on a quiet street, we spied a couple of figures slouched on the sidewalk, propped up against a wall. We were still a small distance away but surmised they were drunk. It appeared to be our first encounter with thoroughly inebriated Cubans. However, when we came close enough to see them clearly, they turned out to be two passed-out Russians.

There were many shops and a number of first-class hotels, comparable to the best in Miami. Outstanding was the twenty-five-story luxury Habana Libre, opened in 1958 as the Havana Hilton. Castro set up his headquarters there in early January 1959. In 1962, it was still practically new and gleaming, its restaurants, bars, shops, and swimming pool offering the best in amenities and service.

Coffee bars were ubiquitous in the early sixties. Cuba's mountain-grown coffee rivaled that of Colombia. It was served thick and sweet in tiny cups. It was superb and cheap enough for mass consumption. Restaurants were plentiful, the food was always tasty, and service was prompt. Rationing of many consumer goods had been introduced in the spring before we arrived. Nevertheless, we were able to find a wide variety of goods, and the quantities were still generous. Miscellaneous merchandise, including clothing, stocked many private shops. We were impressed with the quality and design of the products of Cuba's textile industry.

One of the reasons we were eager to leave Moscow and glad to arrive in Havana was to rescue our teeth. Accustomed in America to semiannual prophylactic treatment, and repair work if needed, we discovered dentistry in Moscow to be in a profound state of underdevelopment. For all practical purposes, it was limited to extraction of teeth and replacement with steel (or gold if you could afford it) "choppers." Very soon after arriving in Havana, we visited a dentist. We found Cuban dentistry to be completely up to date, on a par with American dentistry. It was clear that in this area (and medicine as well), the Soviet Union could have benefited from Cuban technical assistance. In fact, we soon concluded that in matters of consumer welfare and comforts, it was the Soviet Union, not Cuba, that was a Third World country.

\   In other ways, however, arriving in Havana in the summer of 1962 was not good timing. Tension was mounting in the Caribbean, and as a consequence, Soviet-American relations were dangerously deteriorating. Both Moscow and Havana were cities full of tension, but tensions experienced differently. Our anxious Russian friends advised us it would be imprudent to go to Cuba. A second American invasion, following the Bay of Pigs failure the previous year, seemed likely. The mood in Moscow was one of distress and apprehension. Instead of an invasion, however, the climax turned out to be the nuclear missile crisis of October, when only a miraculously fortunate series of diplomatic exchanges prevented an American-Soviet nuclear exchange and the obliteration of Cuba.

In Havana, unbelievably, the popular mood was defiance. "¡Patria o Muerte!" Fidel shouted, and the masses seemed almost eager to take on the Yankees. There was an air of celebration in the city. The Revolution was alive and its driving force was nationalism. It was irrational, to be sure, but nonetheless infectious. Havana was throbbing, and after the dullness and pessimism of Moscow, we were exhilarated, even though, unlike the Cubans themselves, we were apprehensive.

The tenor of Cuban socialism, proclaimed a little more than a year before our arrival, was another surprise. It was officially Marxism-Leninism but modified by the nineteenth-century humanism of José Martí, by the freewheeling mentality of the former guerrillas now in power, and by the cha-cha-cha, the Afro-Cuban popular dance rhythm of the time. In the distinctly Hispanic climate, critical discourse on a variety of topics could take place. Bookstores carried works of competing views and ideologies, including the writings of Leon Trotsky. The Soviet dogma of socialist realism in the arts was ignored. Although many Cuban artists were imprisoned for other reasons, some were celebrated without concern for political ideology. Wilfredo Lam, for instance, Cuba's outstanding surrealist painter, was invited back from Paris and given a hero's welcome in Havana.

Finally, there was optimism concerning Cuba's socialist economy. It built new public housing, lowered the cost of utilities and rent, created thousands of jobs in the new ministries and the armed forces, wiped out unemployment and, with the rationing system and price controls, also abolished inflation. When Anastas Mikoyan, Khrushchev's deputy, first visited Cuba (in February 1960), Che Guevara took him on a tour of the new housing and other public works in progress. Che reported that Mikoyan was astonished, wondered where the money was coming from and remarked that the Cuban Revolution "is a phenomenon that Marx had not foreseen."* Later, it became clear that Cuba's infant social-

* Halperin, *The Rise and Decline of Fidel Castro,* 201.

ism was living off the fat accumulated by Cuban capitalism. Meanwhile, Havana was dazzling and the future seemed bright. It was a far cry from the bleak Moscow we had left behind.

Havana revisited in 1989 on the eve of the thirty-first year of Castro's rule had deteriorated to a surprising degree. A striking example was the change that had taken place in the city's flagship hotel, the Habana Libre. Facing north, the ample balcony of my room on the eighteenth floor still provided a magnificent view of the Gulf of Mexico, but the metal table was rusty and the two armchairs had seen better days. Inside, the furnishings of the room and bath could best be described as Spartan, and lacked a writing desk or floor lamp. The mattresses on the twin beds were thin and worn. A warm current of air flowed from the air-conditioning vent near the ceiling.

The faucet for potable water in the bathroom sink worked sporadically until one day it went totally dry, forcing me to buy bottles of presumably uncontaminated mineral water. About a week after I moved in on November 5, the toilet stopped flushing, though it was quickly repaired. There were clean towels, well worn and probably in short supply because they arrived at unpredictable hours of the day or night. More disconcerting were the cockroaches that cavorted around the sink during the night and that, I soon discovered, infested the entire hotel. The chambermaids, however, were cheerful and joked about the little brown beasts. "You won't be charged for them," one of them said, chuckling. She then sprayed insecticide lavishly around the sink, contaminating my toothbrush, soap, and drinking glass.

In several depressing ways, the basic features of the hotel accentuated its deterioration. The swimming pool, off the mezzanine floor, was a sharp disappointment. I recalled the elegant poolside food and beverage service, comfortable chairs, and bright awnings of years ago. Now there was beer but no shade, and everywhere the eye caught on peeling paint. During half my stay, the pool was closed for repairs. Of the six elevators in the Habana Libre only three were functioning. In a twenty-five-story building, this made for long waiting periods and crowded cars. Waiting in the air-conditioned lobby was not too difficult, though annoying; but on an upper floor, after a long walk in an oppressively hot, musty corridor, a five-minute wait for an elevator was distinctly unpleasant. A particularly depressing demonstration of austerity in socialist Cuba took place in the men's washroom. A third of the urinals were out of order on any given day. Meanwhile, sitting just inside the entrance to the facility was an attendant handing out single sheets of toilet paper to patrons in need. As a twenty-four-hour service, it must have required at least three employees per day. Add weekly rest days, patriotic assemblies, union meetings, and vacation periods, and perhaps toilet paper distribution provided two additional jobs. It was one way for Cuba to maintain its vaunted full employment.

The deplorable telephone service in the Cuba of late 1989 made electronic communication a dreary adventure. To begin with, Havana no longer had telephone directories, reminding me of Moscow in the sixties. The hotel switchboard was helpful in trying to find telephone numbers, but it required time and patience, and usually the operator reported no success. Getting a dial tone was the first obstacle. A second try might produce a busy signal. A third try would likely yield squeaks and squawks. And even when connection was made to an office number (offices usually had two or three non-networked lines, and many individuals had two), reaching the party was problematic. If there were two or more numbers, I would try another line, beginning the whole process over again. I was told that getting a phone repaired in Havana could take weeks or even months. Getting a new phone installed could take years—even in the capital, the nerve center of the country. As far as telephonic communications were concerned, the once modern, efficient Cuba had, by the end of the eighties, slipped back into Third World status.

There had been a complete overhaul of Cuba's telephone system in 1964, as I remember. It was the American AT&T system, installed long before the Revolution and still working well, although beginning to need minor repairs and replacement parts, increasingly difficult to obtain because of the American trade embargo. Castro's solution, as frequently happened, was a drastic one and eminently patriotic: Pull out all the American equipment and convert to "fraternal" Hungarian equipment. I talked to the Hungarian technician in charge of the transfer. He said, "The Cubans are crazy. The American equipment is far superior to ours, even if it is older. It can easily be patched up and kept going indefinitely."*

The rent for my hotel room was $55 U.S. per day, more than it was worth but also an admission that the hotel was no longer the five-star Havana Hilton it used to be. All transactions in the nationalized hotel—restaurants, bars, foreign merchandise shops, the barbershop, and so on— were in U.S. currency. The same was true for the cabs lined up outside the main entrance. One acquaintance told me, half facetiously, "If you have enough dollars, you could buy any hotel in Havana. That's communism." That aspect of Cuba's dual economy is obviously politically embarrassing. It tells the visitor, and indeed all Cubans, that in Havana's major hotels, the national currency is not accepted as legal

---

* "Since the iron curtain lifted last year . . . analysts estimate that the telecommunications network from the Baltic to the Balkans is thirty years behind Western Europe and the United States—a gap that . . . will cost $350 billion U.S. over 15 years to close. . . . It will cost $33 billion U.S. and take six years just to bring East Germany's system up to Western Standards." Dispatch from Budapest to the *Los Angeles Times,* reprinted in the *Sun* (Vancouver, B.C.), Aug. 7, 1990.

tender and that Cuban dependency on the Yankee dollar has survived more than thirty years of Revolution and Marxist-Leninist socialism.

There was, however, a single and telling exception to the rule, a commodity no U.S. dollar could buy. At a tobacco and newsstand in a dimly lit corner of the lobby, only dollars could purchase cigars and cigarettes, but the daily *Granma*, the slender organ of the Communist party of Cuba, sold exclusively for a mere five Cuban centavos. However, the print was faint and the paper extremely thin. Most of the time when I asked for it, it had not yet arrived—or had already sold out. Needless to say, no foreign publications were on sale. The Soviet weekly *Novedades de Moscú* (Moscow News) used to be sold until it was banned from Cuba, earlier in 1989, as a subversive publication, a remarkable sign of the times. I found the same dismal service at newsstands on the street, one of which, however, carried month-old copies of the daily *Pravda* (in Russian). I wondered about efficiency and morale in the critical sector of Cuba's propaganda industry.

The various hotel restaurants ranged from mediocre to acceptable, but most were not up to the standards of the early sixties. Shortages of one item or another on the menus would occur almost daily. Cockroaches lurked in the dark corners. On the mezzanine floor in a large ballroom converted to a self-service cafeteria, the lofty ceiling, from which hung massive, ornate chandeliers, sometimes leaked, especially during hard downpours. On occasion, drops of water from the ceiling would fall into my *café con leche*.

Once I tried to eat at a cafe down the street from the hotel. It was a gloomy spot and the food was inedible, an impossible alternative to the hotel. Another time I tried to get into a Chinese restaurant two blocks from the hotel. Its reputation was better but the line was long. I asked the doorkeeper how long I would have to wait. He glanced at the line and said, "Three hours." There was a Czech restaurant close by and across the street a Bulgarian restaurant—the same story in both cases: several hours of waiting. Thus, the Habana Libre, for all its imperfections, turned out to be an oasis in a consumer desert, provided you had convertible foreign currency.

One thing had not changed. Cubans and others, notably Russians, were constantly smoking cigarettes in the lobbies, in the restaurants, in all public areas of the hotel and, of course, outside. I had quit smoking some years before and more recently had become aware of the dangers of secondhand smoke, which I was unable to avoid. Fidel Castro, once rarely seen without a cigar in his mouth, some time ago had publicly given up smoking. He explained that he had quit to set an example for the people, not out of concern for his own health. Clearly, that was not enough. Nevertheless, there was no antismoking propaganda, visible or audible, of any sort, while the impact of smoking on public health went unreported. Nor was there open questioning of the morality of a virtuous socialist country exporting a product medically certified to be dangerous to health.*

In spite of declining prospects for a clientele of tourists, Cuba nevertheless drew professional groups from all quarters. During the month of my stay, there were at least a half dozen international conferences in Havana. They involved scientific, cultural, commercial, and other organizations. Along with guided tours from many countries, except the United States, they filled the city's hotels, including the Habana Libre. The convention delegates wore the customary badges, and many were accompanied by their spouses. They came mainly from Europe, both East and West, from Japan and Latin America. Most stayed no more than three or four nights, and some then went on to visit seaside communities and their beaches.

The hotel, despite the deterioration from its earlier days, was the center of activity for the groups. I wondered about the reactions of the foreigners to the Habana Libre. Were

---

* Cuban exports of tobacco are actively promoted. They include cigars, cigarettes, and tobacco leaf. To my knowledge, nothing has ever appeared in the Cuban media comparable to the widely reported statement by Dr. C. Everett Koop, former surgeon general of the United States, concerning the sale of American tobacco products abroad. It is, he said, "immoral to be exporting death, disease and disability." *Economist,* Nov. 18, 1989.

they as disappointed as I was? Had they expected more or something different, something less reflective of a decaying system? My best chance to sample opinion came at breakfast time in the large ballroom on the mezzanine floor, the only place in the hotel serving breakfast, a kind of massive communal morning meal. I was thus able to strike up conversations with several visitors. I made every effort to be noncommittal, chatty. "I find the breakfast arrangement here rather odd," I said to a young woman who seemed to be in charge of a group. "I don't recall anything similar elsewhere." It turned out she was leading a tour from Denmark. "Oh," she replied, "they have the same system in Bulgaria. Very practical. And the food is good, like in Bulgaria." A few more questions and answers and I discovered that she and her group were "political pilgrims" (to use Paul Hollander's expression). They had been firm believers in Castro's socialist experiment before coming to Cuba and were not about to change their minds.

I did not share their opinion about the food, particularly the bread. Whatever form or shape it came in, toasted or not, it formed a sticky mass difficult to dislodge from between cheek and gums. I guessed the flour, probably imported from Canada or milled in Cuba from Canadian wheat, was adulterated with something like dehydrated malanga, an African root vegetable abundantly cultivated in Cuba. I used the bread as an opening in a conversation with a husband and wife in early middle age. They came from Buenos Aires where the bread is of legendary quality. "So you are from Argentina," I said. "What do you make of this bread?" Both answered almost simultaneously, "Not fit to eat." I was reminded of Che Guevara's comment about the bread when he reached Havana with his guerrilla column at the beginning of January 1959. "Why can't the Cubans make decent bread?" he asked. The answer then was that most Cubans ate rice, not bread. And when they did eat bread, it was the sliced American-style, sandwich-and-toasting variety. Che could probably never have imagined the deterioration of Cuban bread since those days.

The Argentine couple were definitely not "political pilgrims," so I asked them why they chose Cuba for a vacation. The answer went something like this: A large number of tourist agencies in Buenos Aires are owned by Communists or fellow travelers. They promote Cuba and we fell into the trap. Besides, the Cuba tour is considerably cheaper than any other Caribbean holiday. No, we won't come back nor will we recommend Cuba to our friends.

As for the various international organizations meeting in Cuba, the choice of venue could be a matter of rotation between the member countries but also the result of political choice. For many years the meetings have been eagerly sought by Cuba as proof of status and ability to overcome American blacklisting. Latin American and other Third

World branches of international organizations, as well as Soviet bloc members (prior to 1989), have tended to support Cuban aims. Some years ago, the Cubans managed a large investment in up-to-date convention facilities in Havana, while paradoxically, hotel living quarters declined. From my sampling, I found practically no hostility to the Castro regime among the delegates, with attitudes ranging from ideological solidarity to tolerance. Perhaps most Westerners could be described as curious about Cuba, in a friendly way, ignorant of or insensitive to the darker side of Castro's Revolution, willing to put up with a few days of discomfort in the Habana Libre, but not likely to come back as tourists.

Thus, despite the full occupancy of the Habana Libre and other still viable hotels in Havana, the sad state to which they have been allowed to deteriorate is more than a national disgrace. The formidable financial investment and years of labor that would be needed present a serious obstacle to the restoration of the hotels demanded for a modern tourist industry, and tourism has been assigned a key role in current plans for economic development. The urgency of the problem can be summarized by an article in the *Granma Weekly Review* (May 6, 1990) entitled "Havana Hotels Undergo Remodeling." After mentioning the "advanced state of deterioration of some hotels," it states that "relatively minor work needs to be done on the Habana Libre." If the Habana Libre needed only minor repairs, imagine the state of things elsewhere in the city. How did that come about? The answer is related to a larger urban failure.

\

AT FIRST GLANCE, Havana appeared to have changed little during the quarter century of my absence. Seeing the city again was a real pleasure for me. There was the familiar view of the Malecón, the seaside boulevard bordering the Gulf of Mexico. To the east was the broad Havana Bay with its deep, sheltered harbor (now badly polluted). The tree-shaded campus of the venerable University of Havana and the immense stone staircase—the famous *escalinata*—which leads up to the university on one side, still had their charm. How welcoming and comfortable to find my old parking space next to the building where I used to lecture.

As I walked about the vast Plaza de la Revolución with its massive prerevolutionary monument to José Martí, I recalled joining fifty thousand others in the great square for Fidel Castro's quixotic "Great Supper" of New Year's Eve, 1964. We all simultaneously feasted on the traditional roast suckling pig and fixings for a modest fee. It was an event probably unique since Roman times and hailed by many foreign visitors as a landmark of Cuban socialist achievement. Most of the guests did not know that the rations of the capital's residents had been cut for several weeks to provide some of the food for the supper.

Some twenty-five years later, one new feature of the

Plaza de la Revolución caught my eye. Attached to the façade of a block-long office building was a five-story reproduction of the mournful, bearded countenance of Che Guevara, in vivid color. An oval head of the more heavily bearded Camilo Cienfuegos was superimposed on one corner of the gigantic photo. I had witnessed the beginning of the cult of Che after he was captured and killed in the Bolivian jungles, in October 1967. Since then, the cult of the Argentine hero-martyr has grown to enormous proportions. He has become an icon, exploited as a symbol of the purest revolutionary virtue. Camilo was another hero-martyr, a popular guerrilla *comandante*, presumably drowned in a plane accident in November 1959. Ever since, the anniversary of his disappearance has been commemorated every year.

Others of the city's landmarks were more familiar to me: the Karl Marx Theater, known as the Chaplin Theater in the early sixties, and prior to that called the Blanquita Theater, named after the wife, or mistress, I don't remember which, of the original owner; the ornate National Theater; the stately National Library; the Tropicana Cabaret, still featuring the flamboyant shows of the fifties; and the whole network of streets and avenues that recalled the essential Havana.

Meanwhile, it was evident that very little new construction had taken place during the years of my absence. A new hospital or two, an apartment complex, the International

Conference Center, Lenin Park, and a zoo were scattered over the landscape, along with the ongoing restoration of part of seventeenth- and eighteenth-century Old Havana, a project financed by UNESCO.* The most conspicuous construction under way in Havana, with a top political priority of boosting Cuban revolutionary prestige, was associated with the elaborate preparations for hosting the Pan American Games in 1991. At the same time, the city had approximately doubled in population (two million in 1989), Castro's socialist planning notwithstanding. So many people resulted in congestion and pollution, along with urban neglect coexisting in a now-depressed national economy. Thus, what superficially appeared to be an unchanged Havana was, in fact, a city in lamentable decline.

From the outset, the Hungarian and Czech buses, which replaced the clean, efficient GM vehicles and began to circulate in the streets of Havana in the mid-sixties, were notorious for their lack of comfort and their belching of thick black clouds of exhaust smoke. But twenty-five years later, many more of them coughed fitfully about the city in a bad state of repair. Where traffic was heavy, as in parts of Vedado, or where the streets were narrow, as in Old Havana, breathing could be difficult. There were even times when I could smell the exhaust smoke in my room on the eigh-

---

* In 1982, UNESCO declared the area a world heritage site. The present location of Havana was established in 1519.

teenth floor of the Habana Libre. Adding to the poisonous bus emissions were the thick exhaust gases generated by ubiquitous Soviet Ladas and the dwindling number of old American clunkers of the fifties, which chugged and wheezed through the streets. With the critical lack of repair facilities, most automobiles had to manage without tune-ups, adding to exhaust pollution. In a word, emission controls did not exist in Havana or in the rest of Cuba. It is a problem never mentioned in the glowing accounts of Cuba's public health achievements.

Walking on almost any street, in any part of the city, I was apt to pass a great pile of rubble where a house once stood. Empty stores were everywhere. In some areas, garbage collection was obviously haphazard. Peeling exterior paint seemed to be the norm rather than the exception. In some of the narrow streets of Old Havana, I walked under wooden braces that propped one building against another on the opposite side of the street. In the Víbora residential neighborhood, the stately façades of one-family homes still looked pleasant from a distance. But close up, I could see decay and, once inside, sometimes worse than decay. On visiting one such house, I found that it had been divided into small, dark apartments. The elevator creaked and swayed and seemed to be even flimsier than the elevator of our apartment house on Kutuzovsky Prospekt in Moscow. Inside the two-room unit, light was supplied by a forty-watt bulb hanging from the ceiling. The dilapidated furniture was too far gone to have been accepted by the Salvation Army. The only other source of light flickered on the screen of a 1956 Admiral color television set. The once inviting middle-class houses were still inhabited, but the conditions were deplorable and depressing.

Miramar, facing the Gulf of Mexico, immediately west of Havana proper, was still an attractive suburb of tree-lined avenues, comfortable villas, and low-rise apartment buildings, until examined more closely. One corner of the three-story apartment house on Twelfth Street, probably built in the fifties and where we had lived in the sixties, was now shored up to prevent collapse. What used to be an easy and pleasant stroll to the seaside Sierra Maestra Hotel was now an obstacle course over crumbling sidewalks and puddles of leaking water on both sides of the street. The Sierra Maestra was like an abandoned derelict, in a state of advanced and irreparable devastation. I assumed it was unoccupied until I went inside for a closer look and discovered, to my astonishment, people living among the ruins. I looked for the open-air swimming pool that had once been such an inviting spot. It was still there but bone dry. Once it had been a large pool overlooking the Gulf of Mexico, from which it drew its constantly circulating and filtered seawater. The nearby bar and restaurant had been first-rate accommodations. Like the hotel at the time, the pool's use was restricted to foreign *técnicos*, mainly from the Soviet Union. During our stay in the sixties, my wife and I would walk to the pool several times a week. Poolside, we fraternized with families from Eastern and Western Europe—mainly Poland, Hungary, Germany, Czechoslovakia, and, of course, the Soviet Union—and with a sprinkling of British, French, Canadian, American, and Icelandic citizens. Missing were the Chinese and Koreans; they lived apart in remote protected compounds and were rarely seen in town. They were self-segregated to avoid contamination by what they undoubtedly considered to be the frivolous behavior of Castro's Communists. We played chess and discussed the problems of socialism. A surprising number of East Europeans expressed sharply critical opinions, foreshadowing the Prague Spring of 1968 and the Gorbachev era twenty years later. None of us could have imagined, in our worst nightmares, that socialism would reduce the Sierra Maestra Hotel and its facilities to utter shambles.

By a coincidence, during my 1989 stay in Havana, Fidel Castro made a speech that threw considerable light on the deplorable conditions in the city. Shortly after taking power, Fidel became—and still remains—Cuba's only uninhibited investigative reporter. With nobody to censor or edit or even advise him on what he decides to say in his frequent speeches, and almost never speaking from a prepared text, he often reveals details of the malfunctioning society that otherwise would be hard to come by. When exhorting Cubans to work harder and to correct shortcomings, he apparently feels that, to be effective, he has to be blunt in describing the shortcomings. At the same time, he calculates on gaining the respect and maintaining the confidence of the masses by speaking to them "frankly," "honestly," and "fearlessly." In any event, by spilling the beans, so to speak, from to time he helps the foreign observer partially overcome the deadly, self-righteous, and congratulatory monotony of the Cuban propaganda machine.

The occasion for the particular speech I heard during my 1989 visit was the inauguration of a new construction materials plant in San Miguel del Padrón, a southeastern district of Havana. The purpose was to exhort the workers, organized into crash teams known as "brigades" and the larger "contingents," to adopt "a mental attitude, a moral attitude" to their work, as he put it. His account made clear, however, that their obvious incentives were higher pay, better food, medical attention, and living quarters in exchange for toiling twelve to fourteen hours a day, seven days a week.

To stress the urgency of the work to be done, Castro described the accumulation of Havana's problems. "The unhealthy shanty towns, which had disappeared during the early years of the Revolution, have reappeared," he declared. "The Revolution took great pride in having eradicated the shanty towns." He then spoke of the *ciudadelos*, the decrepit tenements "where families live in one or two little rooms, with very little space." Altogether, he estimated that three hundred thousand people in Havana lived in slum conditions or worse. And to emphasize the predicament of half the city's population, he pointed out that "only 50 percent of our two million inhabitants have proper sewage." He did not mention the health hazard that represented. Instead, sewage problems were linked only to insufficient water supply, which was aggravated by leaking water mains. "Every year," he said, "tens of thousands of leaks are fixed. . . . [They] don't only waste water but flood streets, cause disruption and irritation, ruin the streets, cause potholes," and so on, while "contributing to our transport problem."

Fidel failed to explain the reason for the appalling deterioration of Havana, indirectly blaming the doubling of the population. The fundamental reason was a planning failure, one of many haunting Cuban socialism. Almost as soon as Castro took power, he announced a policy by which rural development would have priority over urban improvement. There was some justification because living conditions in the countryside had long been neglected. Thus, the rhetoric of rural progress became a staple among the "socialist achievements" trumpeted by Castro and his public relations technicians. A new road in the mountains, an apartment house in a remote village, the provision of electric current or indoor plumbing to peasant families, and other items were featured as "triumphs of the Revolution" by Castro and the press. Nevertheless, Castro's government has failed to achieve a major objective of the investment. The Revolution's rural focus has not prevented the movement of the population toward the cities, particularly Havana. Currently, some 70 percent of Cubans reside in urban communities.

And for years, what went unreported was that the favored treatment of the countryside was inevitably accompanied by urban impoverishment. Ignoring maintenance of urban assets was economically counterproductive, amounting over the three decades of the Revolution to a massive decapitalization of the Cuban economy.

Other investments also deprived resources for urban maintenance: large-scale military interventions in Angola and Ethiopia; costly civilian foreign aid support in a dozen Third World countries; full boarding scholarships on the Isle of Youth (formerly the Isle of Pines) for literally thousands of African children, and so on. Whatever the merits, or lack of them, of those undertakings, they contributed to the great burden that the rehabilitation of Havana, and other urban centers, now imposes on Cuba. The misfortune is even greater because the overdue recognition of the problem now coincides with a period of scarce resources during a prolonged general economic depression and dwindling foreign subsidies.

In his speech, Castro went on to list other needs in Havana: bus depots, food warehouses, vegetable markets, bakeries, primary and secondary schools, and more. Still he added, with his customary (but this time hardly convincing) optimism, "We are making tremendous progress." Then a note of caution, a matter of recent concern: "We don't know what the consequences of phenomena now occurring in many socialist countries might be, what direct bearing they will have on our plans, our programs, our economy." And so we must be ready for more sacrifice (after thirty years of sacrifice). "When there are reports of strikes over there," he warned, "you can be sure we run the risk that certain equipment will not reach the country, and we are already suffering some consequences. . . . Certain materials and equipment we are counting on for our plans have been delayed or have not come at all."

There was some irony in the timing of the speech. It was delivered on November 7, 1989, the seventy-second anniversary of the Bolshevik Revolution. Castro dedicated the new plant, the ostensible purpose of the speech, to the memory of Lenin, even as Leninist doctrines were crumbling in nearly every country where they had once been embraced, including the Soviet Union.* With further irony, *Granma* published the full text of the speech on November 9, 1989, the very day the Berlin Wall was breached. That marked the end of the Marxist-Leninist German Democratic Republic, for thirty years a vital source of material and ideological support of the Cuban Revolution.

---

* "His [Lenin's] theories are falling into disrepute, his historic role is being re-examined, and now, in a half-dozen cities around the Soviet Union, his statues are being dismantled, not by bands of hooligans, but by local city councils." *New York Times*, Aug. 26, 1990.

3 ★ *Rice, Beans, and Shoes*

O NE SUNDAY MORNING IN late
November 1989, I took one of the "dollar" cabs
in front of the Habana Libre and arrived unan-
nounced at the apartment of the García family (whose sur-
names and given names I have changed in this book), old
friends of the sixties. I remembered where they lived, but I
did not have their telephone number and knew that trying
to obtain it was hopeless. Even if I had found their number,
there was no assurance the phone would be working. I
hoped that they would be at home and then worried that
they had moved. The latter was unlikely, as I had already
discovered in the case of other old friends. Given the housing situation, there was no place to move to. Those wanting
or needing a change simply patched up the old quarters as
best they could and stayed put.

When I arrived, I found I was in luck. Josefina García
was at home, easily recognizable although now a buxom

housewife in early middle age. After expressing her astonishment, as if I were a returning ghost, she gave me a warm *abrazo*. Alberto, her husband, had taken the car to be repaired by a moonlighting government mechanic. It was a Sunday occupation I well remembered from the sixties. Juanito was there, a small child when I last saw him but now grown up. Shortly, Teresita, his somewhat older sister, came by with her husband. Toward evening, Alberto returned with his repaired ten-year-old Lada sounding like a cement mixer.

The García apartment had two bedrooms, two bathrooms, and a large balcony overlooking a small, pleasant park. The original occupants owned a clothing store in downtown Havana and left Cuba for Israel soon after the Revolution. My friends, I recalled, had been fellow travelers of Fidel Castro's revolutionary movement. They had good connections with the new government when it took over, which paid off when this relatively large apartment was assigned to them. The last time I had seen it, it was bright and cheerful, but now it had a worn look. It was evident that my friends had spent much time and ingenuity repairing it. That was also true of the furnishings that had managed to survive the wear and tear of a quarter century. The only new piece was a Japanese television set, purchased, I was told, from a Russian sailor.

We had a modest dinner and then an even more modest late supper, mainly beans and rice, tastily prepared; and much conversation, mostly about Cuba and its future in the post-cold-war world. The García family were not typical Cubans, to be sure, but they were probably typical of higher income professionals—educated, knowledgeable about Cuba's economic and social problems, and politically sophisticated. Most important, they were candid. The only precaution in their speech that I could detect was that they never uttered the name of Fidel Castro. When they wanted to mention him, they stroked their chins, a silent but unmistakable reference to Castro's beard.

That Sunday, and at a subsequent visit, I concluded that the García family were closet dissidents but did not completely reject the Castro regime. They believed that Cuba needed to "modernize" and "liberalize," as they put it, but should maintain the social services of the Revolution. And in no case should Cuba return to the condition of pre-1959 corrupt American dependency. They agreed that their privately held views did not represent a threat to the security of Castro's regime. The threat, they believed, came from abroad and, contrary to Castro's anti-Yankee paranoia, not from the United States but from the Soviet Union.

A recurring subject in our conversation was the rationing system. Josefina gave me the November food quotas and those for other household necessities. With few exceptions, they were remarkably similar to the allocations Josefina and I remembered of the mid-sixties (in quantities per person per month): five pounds of rice (more about rice later); ten ounces of beans, next to rice the most important item in the Cuban diet; four pounds of sugar, not rationed during my earlier days in Cuba; four ounces of coffee, formerly from superb Cuban coffee beans, now from inferior imported beans while Cuban beans are exported; three-fourths of a pound of beef or pork, bones included; two pounds of chicken, carcass included; half a pound of cooking oil; three small cans of evaporated milk; and half a small can of tomato paste. Fresh fruit, such as oranges and bananas, was available on occasion but only in token quantities. Fish and eggs were normally not rationed and were in reasonable supply. But Cubans traditionally dislike fish, and the customary Cuban preparation of both fish and eggs requires large quantities of scarce cooking oil.

In addition, there were small allotments of soap and toothpaste. Cloth, articles of clothing, and shoes (one pair) were distributed on an annual basis. Alberto showed me the three pairs of shoes he owned. He was wearing the regular rationed pair, obtained three months ago. I doubted the shoes would last the year, particularly since shoe-repair shops did not exist. A second pair, also Cuban made, that he obtained in the parallel market (which I shall shortly describe), cost four times more than the rationed shoes and were obviously of better quality though still roughly finished. The third pair, made in Brazil, he had received from the government on the occasion of an official trip he had taken to Spain. It was a normal pair in quality and fashion, the inexpensive kind, for example, that would be sold by Sears or J. C. Penney in the United States. In addition to his shoes, Alberto was completely outfitted with a new set of imported clothes—suit, shirts, and ties. In Madrid, Alberto would not reflect Cuban austerity. It is government policy (similar to that of other Communist countries) that when a Cuban goes abroad on official business he should appear stylish and prosperous.

Alberto, an agronomist, earned four hundred pesos a month, about twice as much as an average factory worker. He and his wife could, therefore, afford to shop in the so-called parallel market, which did not exist in my day. It was a government-operated system that sold unrationed goods at vastly increased prices. For example, an orange, when available with a ration coupon, sold for thirty centavos (it had been ten centavos in the 1960s). In the parallel market, the same orange, when available, would sell for three pesos, or ten times more than the rationed orange. The parallel market was created to compete with the illegal black market and also to offer some incentive for earning more pesos. According to the García family, the parallel market could provide some relief to an otherwise monotonous diet. For example, the sliced green tomatoes and onions we had at supper were purchased there. But in general, its importance was marginal. The goods in stock would fluctuate wildly in quantity and quality, and most people could not afford to pay the highly inflated prices.

One item on Josefina's list of rationed foodstuffs was particularly significant as a symbol of the historic failure of Cuba's socialist economy. It was the five-pound allotment of rice per person per month. For Cubans, rice, rather than wheat or corn products, has been the preferred grain, the staff of life, since the early nineteenth century when it became the staple food of black slaves. It was nutritious, had been easy to import, and was cheap. Eventually, it replaced bread for the entire population. Only well-to-do cosmopolitan Cubans ate some bread in addition to rice. After World War II, imported rice was difficult to obtain and costly, so Cuban farmers had an incentive to grow rice. In 1949, Cuba produced some 10 percent of domestic consumption. In 1960, the year after Castro came to power, the Cuban rice harvest was four hundred thousand metric tons, making Cuba for the first time practically self-sufficient in rice. During the decade of the fifties, Cuban producers had successfully adopted the latest methods of rice farming employed in Louisiana and Texas. From the point of view of technological expertise, rice production outstripped that of any other branch of Cuban agriculture; and in terms of money value, rice became one of Cuba's major crops.

By 1962, with Cuban agriculture socialized, the rice yield was reduced by 50 percent. That same year, as has already been noted, the rationing of foodstuffs was introduced, with the rice ration set at six pounds per person per month. That lowered the per capita consumption to about two-thirds of what it had been at the time Castro took power. Moreover, for low-income Cubans, for whom rice formed a more substantial part of their diet, the reduction was even greater.

In early January 1966, Castro announced during a long speech that the rice ration would be reduced by one-half, that is, to three pounds per person per month. I remember listening to the speech and wondering whether it would lead to food riots. Castro, however, skillfully shifted the blame. With blistering invective he denounced the Chinese for failing to live up to an agreement requiring them to supply all of Cuba's rice needs in return for massive quantities of Cuban sugar. As Castro explained the deal, its logic assured that there would be mutual "fraternal" benefit with respect to costs and an assured supply of a strategic foodstuff. On the basis of the agreement, which he had personally promoted with a visit to the Chinese embassy in Havana, Castro began to convert rice acreage to sugarcane. The move was in line with his obsession to produce ten million tons of sugar in the 1970 harvest—about double the average harvest since the early fifties.

Thus, in 1965, Cuban rice production had dwindled to fifty thousand tons, a drop of close to 90 percent compared with the banner year of 1960. Rice imported from China made it possible to maintain the six-pound monthly ration until the end of 1965, when the Chinese suddenly terminated the exchange. Castro's public explosion of anger and insult aimed at the Chinese brethren scarcely concealed the fact that he had been extremely naive and imprudent to imagine he could rely on Mao Zedong and company. Their only interest in the deal was political, that is, to obtain Cuban support in their polemic with the Soviets. When Castro failed to deliver the support, they sharply reduced rice exports to Cuba.[*]

The result for the Cuban consumer was a further decline in the already critical shortage of the principal staple of the Cuban diet. It was thus both an economic and a social disaster. Nor did converting the rice acreage to sugarcane prevent the failure of the 1970 harvest to reach the promised ten million tons, which in turn triggered the near total collapse of the Cuban economy. Meanwhile, relations with China did not fully recover for nearly a quarter of a century when, after the great student massacre in Beijing in mid-1989, Cuba ostentatiously accepted the Chinese government's incredible explanation of the tragic event.

Recovering from the rice catastrophe had been a slow and painful process. The five-pound ration at the end of 1989 was still less than the original ration of six pounds set in 1962, itself considerably below average consumption prior to the Revolution. A rare mention in the press of the rice problem occurred in the *Granma Weekly Review* of April

---

[*] For details concerning the rice crisis and Sino-Cuban quarrel, see Halperin, *Taming of Fidel Castro*, 195–207.

2, 1989. It was, of course, upbeat: "Cuba is pushing ahead a program that in the next few years will make itself self-sufficient in rice stocks." It went on to confirm Cuban addiction to rice (contrary to the prediction of some experts that the Revolution could wean Cubans from rice to wheat in twenty years). "Rice," the article stated, is "a grain Cubans can't seem to do without in their daily diet." But the report was also deceitful. "Rice harvesting," it declared, "was practically unknown in the country prior to the triumph of the Revolution in 1959." It was another reminder that purveying misinformation was one of the functions of Castro's press.

IN SOME RESPECTS, sitting at the García table gave me the impression that the clock had stopped twenty-odd years ago: the same round table, the same crocheted tablecloth (an heirloom, no doubt), the carefully preserved tableware, the rice and beans, the entire ambiance of the room. In other respects, time had clearly worked its inevitable changes. To be sure, the Garcías and their children were that much older. Also, Alberto had completed what amounted to a doctorate in the Soviet Union, and he showed me his published dissertation. It was written in Spanish but printed in what was then socialist Bulgaria, of all places. Alberto said that proofreading the copy produced by printers unfamiliar with Latin characters was a nightmare, but there was no other way of getting his book published. Paper in Cuba was in desperately short supply, and so were printing facilities. However, I was also aware that a more important change had taken place. A definite decline in morale could be perceived. When my wife and I said good-bye to the Garcías in mid-1968, there was still optimism about the future of the Revolution. True, there had been hardships, but they were considered temporary. Fidel had promised that Cuba would literally be the best-fed country in the world in just a short time. But austerity persisted, and now the expectation, confirmed by Castro himself, was that it could get worse. To the traditional slogan uttered at the end of his speeches—"Fatherland or death!"— he added a second slogan: "¡Socialismo o Muerte!" ("Socialism or Death!"). It had an ominous ring.

As we sat around the Garcías' table after our late supper, conversation turned to how the family saw, and were affected in their thinking by, the powerful tool of government rationing. Unlike the temporary wartime or emergency necessity accepted by all societies, rationing in Cuba had become a permanent feature of the socialist revolution. I wanted to explore in depth with the Garcías its function and meaning. On the one hand, as Alberto proposed, it was the most conspicuous indicator of a prolonged, systemic economic failure. On the other hand, it was an indispensable device for maintaining social stability and Castro's authority.

In this sense, rationing had been a resounding success, although it should be recognized that without the massive subsidies from the Soviet Union and some help from the erstwhile East European satellites, the rations would have been too slim to satisfy minimum consumer needs. In any event, rationing over the years had provided most of the population most of the time with sufficient proteins, carbohydrates, minerals, and vitamins to maintain normal health.

Alberto estimated that about 60 percent of rationed goods (food and other items) were produced in Cuba. The rest was supplied mainly by the Soviet Union and other members of the now defunct "socialist camp." With the Communist debacle of 1989, maintaining the thirty-year standards of Cuba's rationing system could no longer be taken for granted. The same could be said with respect to Cuba's critical dependency for essential producer goods, especially petroleum. Unlike their expectations during the recurring uncertainties of the Cuban economy in the past, the Garcías now had no confidence in the future.

Meanwhile, Cubans have endured thirty years of accumulated annoyances and irritations. The Garcías complained that lining up for rations once a week, and sometimes more frequently, is time-consuming and hard on the feet. Finding a place in line, or keeping it, can involve shoving, pushing, and even fisticuffs. Not all items for which one has coupons are always available, especially if the customer is close to the end of the line. Although most of the time shoppers bring home enough to eat, most suffer the constant frustration brought on by the absence of choices among produce. As for manufactured goods, the rations are exceedingly skimpy and generally shoddy. Obtaining the right size for shoes and other articles of clothing can mean waiting for weeks or months.

Alberto made another observation about the rationing system that is often overlooked. It is logical for rationed goods to be priced low enough to be within reach of persons on minimum wages. That leads to another logic: If with your minimum wage you can buy all available necessities, and at the same time, there is not much else to purchase even if you have the money, there is no incentive to earn more than your minimum wage. Rationing thus turns out to be one of the potent factors (along with job security and bureaucratic inertia) inhibiting work incentive, which everybody in Cuba, including Fidel Castro, recognizes as a significant obstacle to economic progress. Hence, another paradox of the system: While rationing has been essential for maintaining social and political stability, it has undermined the incentive for increasing income, that is to say, production, which would in turn permit the elimination of rationing.

On the eve of my departure from Havana, I said goodbye to Alberto and Josefina. We embraced and I could see tears in Josefina's eyes. Alberto said, "It's a miracle that we have seen you again. I don't expect another miracle." Neither did I, but I did not reply. It was a moment of deep emotion, and I did not trust my voice.

4 ★ *Perspective on the Political Economy*

M Y PRESENCE IN CUBA IN LATE 1989 coincided with the spectacular disintegration of the Marxist-Leninist-Stalinist systems in the Soviet Union and its East European satellites. The Cuban press reluctantly, and in minimum detail, recorded the profound changes taking place in the Soviet Union, Poland, Hungary, Czechoslovakia, and the then German Democratic Republic. The overthrow of the Romanian despot had not yet occurred. In his speeches Fidel Castro had begun to alert his fellow countrymen to the possible economic consequences for Cuba while insisting that, come what may, Cuba should reject the capitalist backsliding taking place in the crumbling "socialist camp" and remain steadfastly Communist.

The Cubans I talked to, closet dissidents as well as professed *Fidelistas*, reflected the uncertainties of late 1989. What would happen to the already depressed standards of living? Could public-health services, often claimed to be the crowning achievement of the Revolution, be maintained at their present level? Where would the several thousand Cuban students in the Soviet and East European universities and technical institutes be able to complete their studies? There was much black humor about Cuban students shifting to China, North Korea, Albania, and Yemen.

Then there was the question of Castro's much ballyhooed "Rectification of Errors and Struggle Against Negative Tendencies." Inaugurated in 1986, to respond to the faltering economy and to reaffirm Castro's personal authority, Rectification was announced as a campaign to sanitize and invigorate Cuban socialism. It was preceded by an unprecedented removal of top-ranking bureaucrats and Communist party functionaries and was immediately followed by the elimination of the free farmers' markets. The latter, a small concession to private enterprise or "market socialism" (existing in the Soviet Union since the early 1920s), had been permitted to open in 1980. This resulted, as expected, in an increase in the supply of food. As reported to me in my visit in late 1989, there had been complaints that prices were high, but the markets had relieved shortages, for example, of garlic, an often unobtainable staple of Cuban cooking. Castro, however, became alarmed by rumors of "millionaire garlic growers" (his words) and the appearance of a network of profit-oriented distributors and wholesalers. Capitalism, he declared, was rearing its ugly head, threatening the destruction of socialism. More likely,

Castro was primarily concerned about a sector of the economy slipping from state control, that is, his personal control. Without consultation, as was his custom, Castro ordered the free markets abolished.

Although it was not his purpose, Castro's program of Rectification was another admission of the perennial economic failures of Cuban socialism. However, he placed the blame not on the shortcomings of the system but on human failure. He denounced greed and corruption in high places, incompetent and irresponsible managers, lack of discipline in the workplace, ideological backsliding in the leadership, and much more, with the notable exception of his own performance.

Thus, Rectification was not entirely new. It was a replay, on a large scale, of his recurring complaints. I was reminded of a scandal I had witnessed in the spring of 1966. The press carried detailed accounts of how Castro fired Efigenio Ameijeiras, vice-minister of the Revolutionary Armed Forces (FAR), a former guerrilla hero, and Ambassador Raulito Roa. Fidel publicly excoriated them for indulging in what he called the "dolce vita," that is, living it up. I was intrigued by Fidel's naive notion that a political ideology could somehow alter basic cultural attitudes. I spoke at some length about the issue with an official uniquely qualified to offer a perspective from inside the government.

I had known and admired the ambassador's father, Raúl Roa, since before the Revolution. He was an eminent intel-

lectual and Fidel's foreign minister. Raúl Roa had himself
been something of a heretic. He had joined the old Cuban
Communist party in the 1930s but left in disgust over its
Stalinist practices. In 1956, while in exile in Mexico, he
publicly and vigorously denounced the Soviet invasion of
Hungary. He was a master of invective. He was never trusted by Moscow, and during his long tenure as Castro's foreign minister, he was not once invited to visit the Soviet
Union. When I spoke with him about the scandal, he
explained the heart of the problem. "Marxism-Leninism,"
he said, "has not changed the hedonistic culture of these
young Cubans." In other words, traditional Afro-Cuban
tropical culture was resistant to puritanical revolutionary
doctrine. Nor was Marxism-Leninism successful in reorga-
nizing some of Roa's personal habits. When I visited him in
his office, it was in a state of incredible disorder. He
promised to invite Edith and me to dinner at his home. He
never got around to it.

But a purer cynicism about Marxism-Leninism also
existed even during those early years of the Revolution. My
wife and I were once invited to a dinner party at the home
of a cabinet minister. We found an elaborate spread of vin-
tage wines and gourmet delicacies unobtainable in any public market. Noting my surprise as I dipped into the caviar,
my host took me aside and told me with an impish twinkle
in his eyes: "As we all know, when Cuba reaches the stage of
communism, there will be a great abundance of everything.

What we have here is an experiment in adapting to the joys of communism. We are getting prepared for the future."

Castro's remedy twenty years later was the same as in 1966: "revolutionary consciousness," that is, selfless dedication to the high moral goals of socialism and patriotism. But there was one significant variation. This time, Castro promised that unlike on previous occasions when reform was marred by "subjective" errors (meaning his ultraleftist brainstorms of the late sixties), Rectification would not tamper with the basic structure of the Soviet-style planning and management system, which he referred to as the "mechanisms." What Castro very likely had in mind in 1986 was an early warning that glasnost and perestroika, Gorbachev's heresies, would not be tolerated in Cuba. Hence, Castro's Rectification had an additional objective: In contrast to the radical changes under way in the Soviet Union, it was a counterreform dedicated to preserve the traditional Soviet socialist model—as inaugurated by Lenin, perfected by Stalin, and maintained by Brezhnev.

It was the fourth year of Rectification when I arrived in Havana in 1989. Its impact on the economy, in any positive sense, was at best marginal. In fact, it was mainly negative. Economic planning and management had become more rigid, Communist party supervision was tightened, and Castro's direct involvement grew more pervasive. The lack of work incentive was critical and acknowledged as such even by Castro. His remedy, apart from increasingly shrill exhortation, was again a kind of crash program. The regime organized so-called brigades (used earlier but abandoned in the late 1970s), each with a score or two of workers, and contingents (a new formula) involving several hundreds. The members, mainly men but with a sprinkling of women, were volunteers screened by the Communist party for physical and political fitness. They worked from twelve to fourteen hours a day, sometimes longer, under special contracts authorized by the Communist party, running from several months to a few years, and under strict discipline. The work they had performed in their previous jobs was to fall on the shoulders of the plant or office workers left behind. Upon completing their contracts, they were to return to their old jobs, kept open for them. The new "vanguard" workers were supposedly responding to the moral and patriotic appeal of the Rectification drive. They were actually motivated, as in any capitalist society, by material rewards: priority in obtaining new apartments, special food and clothing rations, preferred medical services, and wages three or four times more than the norm. They worked mainly in diverse construction projects and plants producing construction materials. At the time I was in Havana, Castro boasted that more than twenty thousand had already enlisted and eventually two hundred thousand would be incorporated (that would be about 10 percent of the nonagricultural labor force).

Rectification had a disturbing similarity to Castro's crash

programs of the past. It depended on emergency measures that in many cases could not be sustained, were not applicable to most sectors of the economy, and affected many of them adversely. The costs to the economy were thus greater than whatever benefits were obtained. Nobody I talked to, including self-professed *Fidelistas*, could estimate the bottom line. Castro, as usual, provided no accounting information. Instead, he had launched the new slogan, repeated in his speeches and posted on billboards nationwide: "Socialism or Death."* It did not inspire confidence in his rosy reports concerning the great achievements of the brigades and contingents.

Meanwhile, in the shadow of socialist Rectification, Castro was flirting with some of the "mechanisms" of capitalism. For example, a state enterprise known as the Corporación Cimex, S.A., was operating outside the norms of the socialist economy and independently of the National Plan. It had branches in several Latin American countries (the most important one was in Panama before the American intervention in late December 1989) and was engaged in profit-seeking investments, currency speculation, and undercover evasion of the American economic embargo. In Cuba,

---

* In contrast to Castro's stoic attachment to the true faith, Todor Zhivkov, Bulgaria's iron-fisted ruler for thirty-five years, who is awaiting trial for various crimes, declared, "If I had to do it over again, I would not even be a Communist and if Lenin were alive today he would say the same thing. . . . I believe that at its very inception socialism was stillborn." *New York Times,* Nov. 28, 1990.

Cimex owned and managed a fleet of several hundred hard-currency taxis, handled the sale of tickets on the Cuban side for the "unscheduled" Miami-Havana run of Eastern Airlines, and was in charge of the importation of publications from the United States. In a brand-new Varadero Beach tourist hotel jointly owned by the state and a Spanish firm (managed by the latter), Cuban employees who were hired, trained, and supervised by the foreign firm worked without benefit of Cuban labor laws (i.e., could be fired at the discretion of the hotel management). Then there was the large Center for Biotechnology and Genetic Engineering, export-oriented toward the capitalist market and considered a future generator of hard-currency earnings. It functioned with nearly complete autonomy, and its staff of several hundred was treated as an elite corps, with corresponding housing benefits and special access to consumer goods.

Castro's ventures into what could be defined as state capitalism were obviously compelled by a desperate shortage of hard currency. It was a pragmatic move inconsistent with his proclaimed dedication to an unadulterated socialism. The ventures could provide some relief to the currency shortage but could only be marginal in the context of the larger economic crisis. How far is Castro prepared to stretch his pragmatism? Given his mind-set, it would be unrealistic to expect him to dilute socialism significantly with state capitalism. In any event, under Castro, probably no amount of state capitalism would solve Cuba's problems. The state is the main obstacle to progress, and in Cuba, Castro is the state.

It was already apparent at the end of 1989 that, in the context of the changing international scene, Rectification might soon be irrelevant. A new focus was required in evaluating Cuban reality. Can Castro's socialism survive the already faltering, and probably terminal, traditional trade-and-aid relations with the former Soviet Union and Eastern Europe? The likelihood is remote, as a cursory examination of the Cuban experience under Castro will confirm.

TO BEGIN WITH, a widely held misconception related to the Cuban Revolution should be corrected. Contrary to Castro's persistent and self-serving claim, Cuba in the fifties was far from being an underdeveloped country. One could plausibly argue that it was a misdeveloped or semideveloped country, but its economic and social profile was certainly not that of a typical Third World country, such as, for example, Bolivia or Thailand or Angola. The Cuban population, largely of Afro-Hispanic descent, enjoyed a homogeneous culture and spoke one language exclusively. Some three-quarters of adult Cubans were literate, and nearly two-thirds of the population lived in urban communities. That is not to say there was no poverty. Many rural areas suffered from economic backwardness, but it was more like the poverty in Appalachia or the Mississippi Delta than in Haiti. On the other hand, urban amenities in the cities and towns—including potable water, health care, schools, and recreational facilities—were not uncommon.

Cuba's relatively modern development was related to the fact that, as an American economist aptly put it, "From a very early date the Cuban economy developed along capitalist lines." Thus, the subsistence peasant society and other semifeudal features associated with Third World impoverishment were practically absent in Cuba. When Castro seized power, "Cuba's economic institutions were capitalist institutions. . . ." Furthermore, in the late fifties, "The Cuban labor movement, compared with the island's labor force [was] one of the largest in the world."* It was also one of the most advanced. It had achieved the eight-hour day, double pay for overtime, one month's paid vacation, nine days sick leave, and the right to strike. After the Revolution, it lost its autonomy, as well as the right to strike and other benefits. As in the Soviet Union, the trade unions were completely controlled by the state, their main function being to maintain discipline among the workers. That arrangement suited Fidel Castro, apart from the matter of doctrine, because it eliminated the unions as a source of independent power.

When Castro launched his insurrection at the end of 1956, there had been no economic crisis. Property destruction during the guerrilla war was minimal. At the end of the

---

* James O'Connor, *Political Science Quarterly* 19 (1964): 234, 235.

fighting, Cuba's impressive material and human resources were intact. In this respect, I recall a conversation in 1962 with a senior economist of the Central Planning Commission (JUCEPLAN) while he took me on a sightseeing tour of the capital and its suburbs. As we emerged from the recently completed tunnel under the Almandares River, connecting Havana with the Miramar shore, he turned to me and said, "Halperin, if only the Revolution could have been delayed for ten years! We were making great progress in building tunnels, bridges, highways, and factories, and increasing manufacturing and food production." I remember asking whether American investment was responsible. He replied that most of the new development involved native Cuban entrepreneurs and government projects.

Some time later I had a long discussion with René Dumont, outstanding French agronomist friendly to the Cuban Revolution, whom Castro had invited to consult on agricultural problems. Summing up Cuba's rich agricultural resources (soil, sun, rain, and human skills), he said, "With proper management, Cuba could adequately feed five times its current population." After Dumont's second, somewhat critical, book *Cuba: est-il socialiste?* appeared in 1970, Castro denounced him as an agent of the CIA. Nevertheless, after more than three decades of the Cuban Revolution (as Castro still describes his regime, which has long since ceased to be revolutionary), Cuba failed to achieve self-sustaining economic growth. The extent to which it has had a viable economy has been the result of substantial subsidies, primarily provided by the Soviet Union and, in lesser amounts, by the formerly Soviet-dominated countries of Eastern Europe. The subsidies have been in the form of much higher than world-market prices paid for Cuban exports, principally sugar, and much lower than world-market prices paid for Cuban imports—for example, the indispensable petroleum supplied by the Soviet Union. For a few years in the mid-1980s, the Soviet Union even permitted Cuba to export surplus petroleum. While the arrangement lasted, petroleum earned more hard currency for Cuba than any other export sold to capitalist countries, including sugar.

Cuban trade with the erstwhile socialist bloc had another advantage in that it did not involve hard currency, almost always in short supply in Castro's Cuba. At the same time, however, Cuba's limited capacity to earn convertible currency was often a major factor in depressing the economy. That was particularly true during the second half of the 1980s, when a number of important consumer and producer goods could not be obtained from Cuba's socialist suppliers. An added problem at that time was the abrupt refusal by practically all the traditional capitalist suppliers to provide Cuba with credits. Thus, imports required payment in cash.

Other forms of subsidies, such as long-term credits and low interest rates, resulted in a massive accumulation of debt, from time to time leading to postponement of repayment or outright cancellation of debt. Soviet sources, cited by the Mexican daily *Excelsior* (October 17, 1990), reported that the then current Cuban debt to Moscow was the equivalent of $24 billion. There was also the buildup of Cuba's modern and efficient armed forces, with both equipment and training over the years supplied as a gift by the Soviet Union. The best estimate of the total value of Soviet aid during the 1980s, excluding the military component, is between the equivalent of $5 and $6 billion annually, or approximately 20 percent of Cuba's gross national product.[*] Thus, Soviet support for the Cuban economy—politically and strategically motivated until the end of the cold war—was without doubt a determining factor in maintaining its viability, to say nothing of its military capability.

Most Cubans had long been aware of their country's dependence on the Soviet Union, even before its collapse and the end of the "socialist camp." Their attitude, it appeared to me, was a mixture of gratitude and resentment. They saw the Russians as benefactors but generally considered them overbearing and a cultural puzzlement. Their social and personal habits were odd. Their consumer goods were shoddy. I recall how back in the sixties a Cuban housewife complained about Russian canned foods: "Yes, we need them, but whether it's canned fish or meat, it has the same flavor and it's awful." She was right, of course. "I

---

[*] Carmelo Mesa-Lago, "Countdown in Cuba?" *Hemisfile,* March 1990, 7. Professor Mesa-Lago, of the University of Pittsburgh, is a leading expert on the Cuban economy.

always have to add something to remove the curse from the can," she said.

The structural characteristics that eventually led to the profound changes in the Soviet Union and the collapse of the Marxist-Leninist-Stalinist regimes of Eastern Europe are essentially the same that have plagued Cuba. Cuban socialism, however, has had some special features of its own. One is that it has had to contend with the American trade embargo (erroneously referred to as a "blockade" by Cuban propaganda). During the early sixties, it caused such difficulties as the dislocation of trade to distant and unfamiliar markets, a shortage of spare parts for American industrial equipment, the denial of new American technology, and the elimination of tourists from the United States. By the end of the sixties, most of those handicaps were overcome, in large part through expanded trade relations with Canada, Spain, Japan, the United Kingdom, and other capitalist countries. Except for the ban on U.S. tourists (only a trickle manage to visit Cuba), the embargo eventually became an irritant rather than a threat to the Cuban economy. Paradoxically, the embargo has also had some propaganda value. Castro always mentions the "blockade" in explaining Cuba's poor economic performance. He invariably blames Cuba's economic hardships on the "Yankee blockade," diverting attention from his own mismanagement. (In the 1990s he added another culprit, the former Soviet Union and defunct socialist camp.) The embargo also helps to stimulate patriotic animosity against the "colossus of the north" and to convince Cubans that without Castro's adamant refusal to abandon socialism, Cuba would once more revert to being an American colony.

Another special feature of Cuban socialism was the magnitude of Soviet aid, making the difference between survival and catastrophe. I recall that in 1967 or 1968 there was suspicion in Havana that Soviet economic assistance to Cuba was slipping, when compared to aid provided for other Soviet client-states. Marcelo Fernández, minister of foreign trade, asked me to look into the matter. In due time, I came up with a report conclusively showing that, with the single exception of Outer Mongolia, per capita Soviet economic aid to Cuba was consistently several times greater than to any other country.

When speaking of Cuban socialism's special features, one must, of course, speak of Fidel Castro, a unique figure in the socialist world. His personal meddling in the Cuban economy played havoc with the Soviet-style planning and management systems installed in Cuba mainly by Czech technicians. In the late sixties, Castro drastically modified Soviet methods, which he severely criticized as "dogmatic" and distortions of Marxism-Leninism. He created so-called special plans, including, in one case, an export company whose activities went unreported to the frustrated Ministry of Foreign Trade. He appointed the directors himself, and they were personally responsible to him.

His most spectacular undertaking was a crash program inaugurated in 1965 for which he mobilized the whole population, including the military. Its aim was to produce ten million tons of sugar in the 1970 harvest. That would have been double the average annual amount of the previous two decades and would have resulted, in Castro's fantasy, in Cuba's domination of the world sugar market. Combined with this extraordinary effort was an egalitarian, ultraleftist (Lenin would have said "infantile leftist") campaign that gave primacy to "moral" instead of monetary work incentives and abolished practically all private retail trade. Contrary to Soviet, and indeed classical, Marxism, which postulated the building of socialism as a prerequisite for creating communism, Castro announced that Cuba would construct socialism and communism simultaneously.

The 1965 mobilization for sugar production caused huge disruptions in everyday life and might have brought about a rebellion. Many consumer goods and services disappeared. I remember searching in vain for a barber to get a haircut or a cobbler to repair my shoes. They had all been mobilized, along with other urban dwellers, to do "voluntary" labor in the fields. They suffered from the unaccustomed hard work under the blazing sun. Their living conditions were primitive, and they resented being separated from their families, but the penalties for noncompliance were severe, and Castro himself had to set the example by cutting sugarcane—in front of the cameras. Hidden from the cameras was the elaborate tent to which he retired after doing his photo stint.

There was no rebellion, but economic chaos descended with a vengeance. At first, Cubans responded with cynicism and low productivity, not enough to pay for the boots issued to the "volunteers," it was said. A top bureaucrat told how he coped. Put in charge of a cane-cutting brigade, he simulated enormous enthusiasm, shouting commands, gesticulating, urging his laggard workers to fulfill their obligation to the *patria*, while he stood in the shade, waving his machete and avoiding cutting a single stalk of cane. The result was a debacle of major proportions. In 1970, not only did Cuba fail to meet the ten-million-ton goal by a good margin (twenty years later the goal had still not been met by a considerable margin), but the resources consumed in attempting to meet the goal also left the entire economy in ruins. The miracle was that Castro himself survived. However, it left him no choice but to abandon the ultraleftist approaches that his Soviet backers considered heretical. With massive Soviet aid, and the full restoration of Soviet planning and management "mechanisms" (Castro's terminology), the Cuban economy was rebuilt during the course of the 1970s.

In addition, for the first time since Castro came to power, both the Cuban Communist party and the Cuban state were "institutionalized," according to the then existing Soviet norms. The First Congress of the Communist party took place in 1975, that is, ten years after the party's formal creation. The next year a constitution was adopted, some twenty years after Castro had promised to restore the liberal constitution of 1940, set aside by Batista. The new constitution, however, bore no resemblance to the one he had promised to restore. Like the reorganization of the Communist party, it closely resembled the corresponding Soviet model, which it explicitly acknowledged as its inspiration.

There was a certain amount of irony in the institutionalization of the Cuban Revolution. It was the first time Castro fully accepted the Soviet models, for both the Cuban economy and the Cuban state. The rationality of those models, however flawed, for several years restrained Castro's impulsive improvisations and provided a new stability for the Cuban economy. During the first half of the 1980s, living standards, excluding housing, improved modestly. The irony was then compounded when Gorbachev's reforms began to transform the Soviet Union. Once more, as during the sixties, Cuban policy began to diverge from that of the Soviet Union. But this time, it was Castro who defended the old Stalinist order while the new Soviet leadership began to transform it.

REVIEWING THE CUBAN experience under Castro makes clear that despite the fluctuations in Cuban-Soviet relations, in the last analysis what sustained the Cuban Revolution over the years was the economic and political underwriting of the Soviet Union. The critical dependence of the economy on the Soviet Union and the erstwhile socialist bloc, the latter compelled by Soviet dictate to contribute to Cuba's survival, sheltered Cuba from the storm of economic collapse. However, with the end of Soviet compulsion, the former bloc members at once began to eliminate preferential treatment of Cuba. In fact, the Eastern bloc, practically as a manifesto of their independence, at the Geneva meeting of the United Nations Human Rights Commission in March 1990 committed the unthinkable. For the first time, Poland, Hungary, Czechoslovakia, and Bulgaria voted with the United States, and against Cuba and the Soviet Union, on a resolution requiring continued scrutiny of human rights violations in Cuba.

An enraged Castro publicly denounced his former fraternal trading partners and revealed some long hidden skeletons in the socialist closet. In a speech on March 7, 1990 (carried in *Granma Weekly Review*, March 18, 1990), he particularly lashed out against the shoddy goods they "dumped" on Cuba. "There's one thing I want to say here, and say it clearly once and for all," he declared. "There is some junk that only we buy [from these countries]. . . . I'll give you an example: we were the only ones in the world who bought Bulgarian forklifts. They're so worthless and have so many problems. . . . There are hundreds, even thousands of these forklifts standing idle in our warehouses," and so on. He then turned to the Hungarian buses. They only get "six kilometers to the gallon," about half of what they should get. "They fill the city with exhaust fumes, poisoning everybody. We could draw up the statistics on how many people the Hungarian buses kill." Finally, he summed up, "A large chunk of what they produce, only we buy from them. . . . We're exporters of [good] foodstuffs and raw materials and we often received in exchange this kind of junk I'm telling you about. . . . I'm glad I'm now able to speak so freely; let's forget about scruples."

It would seem that Cuba, exchanging wholesome sugar and quality nickel concentrates for "junk," was the benefactor of the socialist camp rather than vice versa. However, Castro forgot other imports from Bulgaria, such as large quantities of critically needed processed foodstuffs and various types of farm machinery and implements, perhaps not up to capitalist standards but perfectly serviceable. As for the Hungarian buses, they were the only ones that could be obtained without hard currency and, for all their defects, have carried millions of Cubans every year since the middle sixties. On the other hand, after lambasting a Czech component of the Hungarian buses, Castro did acknowledge the value of Czech imports: "We bought Czech thermoelectrical plants. . . . It wouldn't be fair to say that the Czech thermoelectrical plants are bad, for they're rather good." Then he added that unfortunately the Czechs can no longer be trusted: "But who will guarantee us the spare parts we need for the Czech thermoelectrical plants?" Castro did not say so, but here was a much more important matter than the

Bulgarian forklifts. The Czech contribution to the Cuban economy was substantial and, as in the case of the thermo-electrical plants, vital.

As for the Soviet Union, Castro flashed the first signal of changing relations with Cuba in late December 1986. Commenting on a million-ton shortfall in sugar production, he revealed that unaccustomed pressure was being applied to Cuba by the Soviet Union to meet its sugar obligations. "We can no longer do what we did at times before," he explained, "simply reduce our deliveries to them so as not to affect our deliveries to the capitalist market." As a result, he continued, in 1987 Cuba would have only "half the traditional sum for hard currency expenditures."* It was an astonishing and catastrophic reduction of purchasing power in the capitalist world.

Nevertheless, unlike his bitter attack against the lesser members of the socialist bloc, his public response to the Soviet ultimatum was polite, almost deferential. On various occasions he would explain that although Soviet reforms were not suitable for Cuba, he respected the Soviet Union and understood that its difficulties in continuing to meet Cuban needs were due to its internal problems and not to a deliberate change in policy. Uncharacteristically, he chose prudence rather than invective, recognizing the supreme

* Speech delivered at the second session of the National Assembly, *Granma Weekly Review,* Jan. 11, 1987.

importance of good relations with Moscow and, no doubt, hoping for the failure of Gorbachev's perestroika and Moscow's return to the status quo ante.

During my 1989 stay in Havana, at the still comfortable villa of a former top functionary, I exchanged views with him and his wife on the "Cuban condition." It became evident that Gorbachev's new policy concerning sugar imports from Cuba was the straw that broke the camel's back. The Soviet move brought on the severest economic crisis since Castro came to power. Not only did Cuba suffer the dramatic, and what became a continued, reduction in hard-currency revenue; in 1987 and 1988, Cuba also had to purchase one million tons of sugar (the equivalent of about 15 percent of Cuban production at the time) from capitalist sources to meet commitments to the Soviet Union.

And what about the future of Cuban socialism? I asked. Theoretically, my friend the ex-functionary replied, it could survive the current crisis. We could substitute oxen and human labor for tractors and bulldozers, use bicycles instead of automobiles, drastically reduce the consumption of electricity, and transfer thousands of urban residents to the countryside to produce food. In other words, he added, "instead of moving into the twenty-first century, we would move back into the eighteenth. Of course, it won't work, and I don't have to tell you why."

Within a year, my government-official friend was proved accurate in his vision. Castro set out to do exactly what my friend had hypothesized, as reported in the *New York Times* of December 1, 1990. Calling it a "special period in time of peace," and with Soviet supplies of oil running about 20 percent less than in 1989, Castro began sending Havana office workers to state farms "for three week stints. . . . By March [1991] as many as 18,000 Havana residents . . . will be deployed at any given time at the sixty simple barracks-like camps being rapidly built . . . in the rich lands of Havana Province." Other measures taken were extending the list of goods to be rationed, closing the near empty parallel markets, and eliminating lunch breaks in Havana offices so that the personnel would leave by 3:00 P.M. to save electricity. Furthermore, the plan called for "widespread substitution of oxen for farm machinery and hundreds of thousands of bicycles, already on order from China, for gasoline-consuming vehicles."

Cubans on bicycles indeed mark a significant turning point in the history of Marxism-Leninism in Cuba. I do not recall seeing a single adult Cuban on a bicycle in Havana during the entire period of my residence in the city from 1962 to 1968. As a matter of fact, in 1959 there were more privately owned passenger cars per inhabitant in Cuba than in Spain or Portugal and almost as many as in Italy.*

---

* Approximately 1 car per 32 inhabitants in Cuba; 1 per 51 in Portugal; 1 per 102 in Spain. In Italy, the ratio was 1 to 23. Calculated from tables on Population and Motor Vehicles in Use, *United Nations Statistical Yearbook* (New York: United Nations, 1960).

My friend was no prophet, only an astute and honest observer of the system he struggled to serve. His vision of the decline of Cuban society and culture had been offered dispassionately, without bitterness and without the recrimination-laden tones of a disappointed and once naive enthusiast of the Revolution. He was reflective, pragmatic, and unfortunately, exactly right.

5 ★ *Portrait of a Loyalist*

ONLY AT THE VERY END OF MY STAY in Havana did I locate and get a message to Marcelo Fernández. He promptly phoned me and early one morning came to visit me at the hotel. It was December 5, 1989, and I was due to leave for Miami late that night. I would have been very much disappointed had I failed to see him. Although I was not an intimate friend, I had seen a good deal of Marcelo when I served as his consultant after he became minister of foreign trade in 1964. Among the high-ranking functionaries I knew, I considered him a model of dedication, sober judgment, and professional integrity. He was then in his mid-thirties. He had been a student at the Massachusetts Institute of Technology but had returned to Cuba to head Castro's underground support movement during the insurrection.

Although the underground played a crucial role in the triumph of Castro's guerrilla forces, the full story has never been told to this day. When Jean-Paul Sartre visited Cuba in

1960, he talked with a number of the veterans of the underground and wrote about it in his book *Sartre Visita a Cuba* (the Spanish version appearing in Havana in 1961). He described how those clandestine fighters engaged in sabotage and supplied indispensable weapons, ammunition, food, and money to the guerrillas in the Sierra Maestra. He concluded that the bravery of those who faced the perils of the underground was "more difficult than military heroism: a lonely struggle without witnesses against an all-powerful enemy," with a fate worse than death if they were caught.

Marcelo was probably a hero, but he never talked or wrote about his exploits. I attributed that to his modesty. Later I learned that Castro in fact "discouraged," as it was put to me, publicity concerning the underground exploits. It could diminish the exclusive role he wished to attribute to his guerrilla troops, and their inspired leader, in the overthrow of Batista's government. However, he did reward Marcelo. After Che Guevara's brief tenure as Castro's first president of the National Bank of Cuba, he appointed Marcelo to succeed Che. At the same time, Marcelo, along with other anti-Communists participating in the insurrection, followed Castro in accepting Marxism-Leninism.

It was early in 1964, as I recall, that I was introduced to Marcelo. At the time, he was running the National Bank and, in that capacity, was a member of Castro's cabinet. After a short conversation, he invited me to be an *asesor*, that is, consultant in his office. The reason I did not immediately accept was that I was to see *Comandante* Alberto Mora, minister of foreign trade, that very afternoon, and I suspected he might make me a similar offer.

Mora turned out to be an even younger man than the youthful Marcelo, with a bigger job and less preparation for it. When I left his office late in the afternoon, I was the *comandante's asesor*, and was to report for work the next day. The following morning, as I was walking along the corridor leading to the minister's office, I ran into Marcelo, who was heading in the opposite direction. I greeted him with embarrassment, explaining that I had accepted an offer similar to his from Alberto Mora. "The Ministry of Foreign Trade is a larger and more complex organization than the bank," I explained, "and it offers more scope for whatever talents I have. It would have been a pleasure to work with you, but under the circumstances. . . ." He cut me off, and I remember the strange smile on his face. He was clearly not offended. "I understand," he said. Then he added enigmatically, "We'll be seeing a good deal of each other very soon." We shook hands, and I continued on my way to Mora's office, deeply puzzled.

I walked into the office and discovered to my astonishment that Mora was no longer minister of foreign trade. The new minister was Marcelo Fernández, who left word to inform me that I was invited to remain in the ministry with the same function agreed upon with the former minister.

Later I learned from Mora what had happened. An hour

or so after I had left him, he was urgently summoned to see Castro, with no suspicion about what was to take place. Castro severely berated him and fired him on the spot. Only a month earlier Castro had attended his wedding. The hapless Mora, like others who had had Castro's favor and then lost it, disappeared into the anonymous ranks of the labor force. A year or so later he committed suicide. It was the second and final tragedy to strike the Mora family. Alberto was the son of Menelao Mora, a martyr in the struggle against Batista. He was a principal organizer of the failed attempt by the student Directorio Revolucionario to assassinate Batista on March 13, 1957. Menelao was one of the leaders in the assault on Batista's residence. He was killed in that action. The anniversary of the "attack on the palace," as the event is called, has been officially commemorated in Cuba ever since the triumph of the Revolution. I had heard stories of Castro's arbitrary impulses and of his insensitivity to the atrocities committed against suspected subversives in the overcrowded detention centers in Havana. His brutal treatment of Alberto Mora, a friend and loyal functionary, confirmed for me the darker side of Castro's personality.

Still, working for Marcelo Fernández was a pleasant assignment. He had a cheerful disposition and was quick to grasp the fundamentals of his job. He resisted the dogmatism of both the old-time pre-Castro Muscovite Communists and the new utopian leftists, among them Che Guevara, with whom he engaged in a hard-hitting public polemic in 1964. This concerned what, at the time, had become a major issue, namely, the correct Marxist method of economic planning and management. During the six years I spent in Cuba, I was careful to maintain a strict neutrality in higher policy matters. There was one exception: the Great Debate of 1964. I decided it was important to support the liberal side.

I wrote an article entitled "Hacia un Nuevo Sistema de Planificación y Dirección Económicas en la Unión Soviética" (Toward a New System of Economic Planning and Management in the Soviet Union), published in the October-December 1964 issue of *Comercio Exterior*, a quarterly journal of the Ministry of Foreign Trade. I was identified as "Profesor de Geografía Económica en la Universidad de la Habana." The article described and supported the proposals for economic reform in the Soviet Union made by Yevsei Lieberman, a professor at the Kharkov Technological Institute. Known as the Lieberman Plan, it was first published in *Pravda* in the fall of 1962 and for several years was widely discussed in the Soviet Union and Eastern Europe.

In essence, it made three points: (1) current economic planning and management practice did not meet the needs of the Soviet Union; (2) the remedy was decentralization of decision making and management; and (3) profitability should be the measure of economic success and distribution of rewards. The Lieberman Plan reflected the anti-Stalinist thaw of the Khrushchev period but was never implemented, thus delaying the needed reform of the Soviet system for a quarter of a century until the Gorbachev era. I did not in so many words propose that Cuba adopt the Lieberman Plan, but I clearly implied as much. As a result, the article attracted attention and its author was labeled by both Stalinists and Che Guevarists as a "revisionist," that is, deviating from the true Marxist-Leninist doctrine. In sum, I had been rejected as a foreigner meddling in Cuban internal affairs. I was, therefore, enormously gratified one day when Marcelo stopped me in the corridor. "I enjoyed your article," he said, and moved on.

Why Castro allowed the year-long open debate on economic policy and ideology to take place is still a mystery. He remained uncharacteristically aloof before finally putting a stop to it. At the same time, he inaugurated his own version of a "purified" and "revolutionary" Marxist-Leninist system, as if the long debate had not occurred. In Cuba, to be pro-Lieberman or anti-Lieberman turned out to be irrelevant. Castro made all the decisions.

In 1965, Castro renamed his ruling United Party of the Socialist Revolution (PURS) the Communist Party of Cuba, a name proclaiming a militant commitment to the fundamental principles of Marxism-Leninism. At the same time, there was a reorganization of the party, including the creation of a central committee, whose members, in other Marxist-Leninist states, were normally elected at a party congress but in Cuba were appointed by Castro. (Actually the first party Congress did not take place until ten years later, in December 1975.)

When the list of some one hundred members of the Central Committee of the Communist party of Cuba was published, the name of Marcelo Fernández was among them. I was in his office soon after and congratulated him, adding, "Marcelo, now that you are a member of the Central Committee of the Communist party of Cuba, don't you think you ought to learn something about Marxism-Leninism? I'll be glad to help you." He blushed, laughed, and mumbled something but took no offense. He had a good sense of humor and, in effect, admitted that he knew little about the guiding doctrine of the state. That was probably true of most of Castro's Central Committee in 1965. They were nominally Communists but mainly *Fidelista* loyalists and members of a new bureaucratic elite. The last time I had seen Marcelo was toward the end of 1967. He summoned me to his office one day and told me there had been complaints that I was making critical remarks about Marxism and the Cuban Revolution. As I recall, they were in fact only mildly skeptical comments, intended to be humorous. Marcelo seemed to be somewhat embarrassed and talked in a low voice: "We have some new *comecandelas* [firebrands] in the Ministry, and it would be best to be prudent in your conversations."

I had already noticed a new mood of security and doctrinaire conformism in the press, the ministry, and the university, where I was giving a course in economic geography. A woman teaching in the geography department had suddenly disappeared about that time and then, just as unexpectedly, later returned. Everybody in the department pretended not to notice her absence or reappearance. I presumed she had been picked up by security, interrogated for several weeks, and released. Later, I learned that in some cases an absent academic would never return.

In early January 1968, the head of the Personnel Department informed me that my job at the Ministry of Foreign Trade was to be abolished. It was nothing personal, he said. There was a new government policy that foreigners could no longer occupy "sensitive" positions. My wife and I left Cuba soon after.

ON DECEMBER 5, 1989, Marcelo showed up promptly at 9:00 A.M. in my room at the Habana Libre. Now in his late fifties, he had changed very little in the nearly quarter of a century that I had not seen him. A man of medium height, his hair only slightly gray, with a rather large forehead and slightly florid complexion, he was wearing a conservative business suit of good quality. He gave the impression of a comfortably situated executive of a large corporation or perhaps the director of a scientific research center, seemingly remote from the material austerity and intellectual deprivations of the Cuban Revolution.

We talked until noon, sometimes in Spanish, sometimes

in English, in which he was perfectly fluent. Though neither of us mentioned it, both of us knew any hotel room occupied by a foreigner would be bugged, and that made part of our conversation resemble a friendly, leisurely fencing match. I would ask mildly provocative questions about Cuba's current economic crisis or international relations, and he would give the "right" answers but with sophistication and an air of resignation. Yes, changes in the Soviet Union and Eastern Europe were creating trade difficulties, but we could probably continue to do business, perhaps on the basis of annual instead of five-year agreements. No, we couldn't afford glasnost and perestroika in Cuba as long as we were threatened by the implacable hostility of the United States. He laughed when I quoted what Jacobo Timerman, the Argentine journalist, had written in an article a year or so earlier: "In Cuba everybody has a job, but nobody works." True, he said, incentive to work is our number one problem. On this point, he was on safe ground because Fidel had repeatedly said pretty much the same thing.

Marcelo had been minister of foreign trade from 1964 to 1980. At the end of his tenure, there had been speculation in the Western press that Castro had fired him for reckless spending on hard-currency imports. He had another explanation: "I told Fidel that sixteen years as minister were enough, and he accepted my resignation." And what about Fidel? I asked. Weren't Fidel's thirty years as Cuba's *Jefe Máximo* (Supreme Leader) enough? "Fidel is not an ordinary person," he replied. "His leadership has been and remains indispensable." In any event, Marcelo Fernández did not share the fate of his predecessor, Alberto Mora. Though in time Marcelo was dropped from the Central Committee, he had held a number of well-paying jobs. Currently, he was a consultant to the Central Economic Planning Committee and also lectured at the Higher Institute of International Relations. I went down with him to the hotel entrance to see him off. A car and driver were waiting for him.

What prompted Marcelo to come and see me? I was gratified to think that he had a high regard for me. He also was eager to present me with an inscribed copy of his recently published book *Cuba y la economía azucarera mundial* (Cuba and the World Sugar Economy). He was obviously proud of the book, his first, although for years he had been Cuba's leading expert on the topic. At the same time, he knew I had written critically of the Castro regime. "In your next book," he told me, "don't use the kind of terrible titles you gave to your previous books on Cuba." Surely, it seemed to me, he would not have visited me if Cuba at the moment was in a period of severe repression. It is true, as I had noticed, that a few active dissidents were going to jail, though not for the traditional twenty- to twenty-five-year terms so common in the earlier days of the Cuban Revolution, but for three to five years. Although the security police were still in business and their amateur collaborators, the block leaders of the ubiquitous Committees for the

Defense of the Revolution, were still vigilant, the atmosphere suggested not a reign of terror but one of self-imposed prudence. Marcelo could visit his old American consultant, mind his words, and feel reasonably secure.

I thought about Marcelo, still loyal to Castro, years after the glamour and hopes of the Cuban Revolution had faded. Other younger loyalists I had met during my visit had benefited from the social mobility created by the Revolution and were frank to tell me they owed a debt of gratitude to Fidel Castro. For example, a bright analyst, probably an infant when Castro took power, who worked in the *Centro de Estudios sobre América* (Center for American Studies, a Communist party think tank) made it a point of letting me know he was the son of a cab driver. Then there was the black university professor who, in defending the Cuban Revolution, also referred to his family background. He was the son of a sugarcane cutter, at the bottom of the social ladder before the Revolution.

Marcelo, on the other hand, came from a well-to-do middle-class family. He could afford to be educated in the United States. He was clearly a man of rational disposition. He was completely aware of what was going on in the world at large. As former minister of foreign trade, he knew more intimately than most the causes and extent of the thirty-year failure of Cuba's socialist economy and Fidel Castro's personal involvement in the failure. At the same time, if he had been asked, he could probably have justified his long years of collaboration with Castro.

When he joined Castro's movement, at great personal risk, he had no idea that the elimination of the corruption and crimes of the Batista dictatorship would lead to another dictatorship, perhaps more benign in some respects but also more oppressive in others. He had not expected socialism, but he could accept it because it came with nationalism, that is, an assertion of economic and political independence from the United States, the goal of Cuban patriots for a half century. When the true nature of Castro's authoritarian orientation revealed itself, Marcelo might have chosen to oppose it or go into exile, as many did. Instead, he accepted a cabinet appointment, and all its perks, probably with a clear conscience. It was a well-deserved reward for his contribution to Castro's successful insurrection. At the same time, he could further rationalize his loyalty to Castro, who, through all those years, still retained the aura of the champion of the people's welfare and defender of Cuban nationalism.

And what realistic alternative did Marcelo have? The masses by and large still believed in the charismatic commander in chief. His machinery for control and repression was formidable. Marcelo, who in his youth risked his life for the Revolution, was understandably in no mood to risk it again, this time for a probably hopeless cause. Hence, Marcelo and other intrinsically sober Cubans like him, who have the intellectual capacity to rescue the country from its economic and political bankruptcy, have silently coexisted in the Cuban Revolution with the opportunists of the Communist party and the obsequious bureaucracy that manages Castro's dictatorship. Perhaps that explains why no outstanding Cuban writer, scientist, or other professional, still living in Cuba, thus far has spoken eloquently in defense of human rights and democratic reform as have the Soviet Union's Andrei Sakharov or Czechoslovakia's Vaclav Havel.

6 ★ *On the Sugar Treadmill*

CHRISTOPHER COLUMBUS "DISCOV-
ered" Cuba on his first voyage in 1492. The
Spaniards who occupied the island introduced the
cultivation of sugarcane in 1512. Soil and climate favored
the growth of the new plant, but it was not until the nineteenth century that its potential as a source of wealth was
realized. The end of Spanish rule in 1898 eliminated the
political obstacle to growth. At the same time, a great worldwide increase in demand for dietary sweetness, major
improvements in the technology of sugar production and
maritime transportation, and the influx of large quantities
of investment capital, mainly American, coincided to bring
about the rapid advance of Cuba's sugar economy.

Until Fidel Castro came to power, sugar had been, by
and large, a positive factor in the economic growth and
modernization of Cuba. As Marcelo Fernández points out in
his book *Cuba y la Economía Azucarera Mundial,* the steam

engine had begun to replace oxen as a source of power in Cuban sugar mills as early as 1827, and the first steam-driven railroad line to transport sugar was built in 1837, shortly after the railroad appeared in the United States.* As sugar cultivation moved eastward from Havana across the island, so did an infrastructure of transport, seaport, and maintenance facilities, followed by thriving commercial centers, increased tobacco, livestock, fruit and vegetable production, and various light industries.

However, the sugar-based economy also had negative aspects. Conspicuous among the latter was the constant, and sometimes wild, fluctuation of the price of sugar on the world market, reflecting changes in supply and demand and commercial speculation. Thus, there were periods of prosperity followed by periods of depression. However, under Castro, according to Harvard professor Jorge Domínguez, "Cuba's response to economic prosperity has . . . been problematic. In each of the three world sugar price booms since the early 60s, Cuba has mishandled its economic policies, over imported, and generated the foundations of a subsequent economic crisis."**

When I originally arrived in Havana in 1962, two years

---

* (Havana, 1989), 157. Subsequent page references in this chapter are to this source.
** Jorge I. Domínguez, "The Obstacles and Prospects for Improved U.S.-Cuban Relations," in *U.S.-Cuban Relations in the 1990s,* ed. Jorge I. Domínguez and Rafael Hernández (Boulder, Colo.: Westview Press, 1989), 32.

after Cuban sugar plantations and sugar mills were nationalized, the Castro regime had embarked on a program to abol-
ish monoculture, the term used by Latin American
economists to describe excessive dependence on a single
export commodity. The plan called for the diversification of
exports, import substitution, and at the same time the rapid
development of Cuban industry, in particular heavy industry (the latter was an obsession of Che Guevara). However,
in a very short time the plan turned out to be an irrational
undertaking. It was doomed by a lack of expertise and
resources, compounded by planning and management failures of the new socialist system.

In mid-1963, with Soviet urging, the plan was abandoned. Export diversification, import substitution, and
heavy industry became long-term, slow-moving goals, and
sugar was restored to its preeminent role. Following the
break in relations between the United States and Cuba in
1961, the Soviet Union became the principal market for
Cuban sugar. An agreement was reached with Moscow for
annual deliveries of sugar at stable, above-world-market
prices. Unlike the previous preferential price arrangement
with the United States, Soviet imports of Cuban sugar were
to be paid for in rubles, a nonconvertible currency. It was
something like a barter agreement, with Cuba exchanging
sugar for Soviet goods. The same type of barter trade was
adopted in the exchange between Cuba and the East European satellites. The effect was that the Cuban economy

became more dependent on the Soviet Union and the socialist bloc than it had once been on the United States. That dependency produced another disadvantage: Because bartering meant that Castro's government had little in the way of convertible currency, which turned out to be critical in later years, Cuba was deprived of high-quality and sometimes essential goods in the capitalist markets.

Nevertheless, the theory of the plan was attractive. Castro and his Soviet advisors assumed that the new emphasis on sugar exports would solve the problems of the lagging socialist economy and promote its growth. The success of the restored monoculture would be guaranteed because it took place on the bases of presumably scientific planning, fair and equal exchange, and the high ethical principles of Marxist-Leninist socialism. It was also heralded as an example to the Third World afflicted with the chaos and greed of the capitalist trading system.

However, "life itself," as the Russians say, soon proved that the new plan was seriously flawed. A main problem was the inability of Cuba's inefficient nationalized sugar industry to maintain enough output to meet the commitments to the Soviet Union. Before the introduction of mechanical cane cutters in the 1970s, 350,000 laborers were required for the harvest. In 1989 only 60,000 manual workers were needed. By that time, three-fourths of the crop was harvested mechanically. But the mechanical cane cutter, which the Kremlin promised in 1963 for use by 1965, did not materialize until the late 1970s. Thus, when the first six-year plan ended in 1970, sugar deliveries to the Soviet Union fell short by nearly 50 percent.[*] Among other consequences, the shortfall contributed to a serious strain in political relations between Cuba and the Soviet Union during the late sixties.

By that time, Cuban-Chinese relations also had deteriorated. In 1966, a sugar-for-rice deal personally proposed by Castro had collapsed, with Castro publicly accusing the Chinese of double-crossing him. Rice rations had to be drastically reduced and remained reduced into the 1990s. Only after Cuba publicly accepted the Chinese explanation of the Tiananmen Square student massacre of June 1989 was cordiality restored.

Ironically, on January 3, 1969, the day after the tenth anniversary of Castro's rule, the unimaginable happened: Sugar was rationed in Cuba. To my knowledge, it remains so even now. The climax to the ill-fated sugar revival, however, came in 1970. Castro himself had taken charge of a desperate effort to produce an incredible harvest of ten million tons. He had mobilized the entire population, including the military. Actually, some eight million tons were produced. It was the largest sugar harvest in Cuban history, but in the process the entire Cuban economy was wrecked. The wonder was that Castro himself survived.

[*] Halperin, *Taming of Fidel Castro,* 292.

Meanwhile, Cuba had accumulated an enormous debt to the Soviet Union with no prospect of repayment. Castro had no choice but to accept massive Soviet aid to restore the shattered Cuban economy and finally to institutionalize the Revolution on the Soviet model. In so doing, Castro acknowledged his inevitable dependence on the Soviet Union. Cordiality was restored between the Communist center and its Cuban periphery.

In the fifties, sugar represented about 75 percent of the value of Cuban exports. When I left Cuba in 1968, it was something more than 75 percent. When I returned at the end of 1989, it was about 80 percent and has remained at that level during the early nineties. Thus, Cuba's traditional dependence on sugar exports for acquiring essential imports has remained practically unchanged during the thirty-odd years of socialism. It would appear to illustrate the classic French dictum about apparent change: "Plus ça change, plus c'est la même chose." But there was a difference. Unlike the presocialist era, sugar exports in the aggregate during the Castro period often went to the wrong markets and were not sufficient to provide Cuba with the imports needed for self-sustaining economic growth.

That fact was underscored after the extraordinary events of 1970. To be sure, a degree of rationality and stabilization was achieved in the sugar industry. Cuba even saw a gradual increase of production from about 5 million tons per annum in the early seventies to some 7.5 million tons on the average in the late eighties. That figure translated into annual exports of some 7 million tons, of which about a quarter went to capitalist markets. The latter was crucial because it was the source of convertible currency.

However, in only three of the fifteen years between 1971 and 1985 was the average annual U.S. dollar price on the world market something over twenty cents a pound (the last time in 1980). In the other twelve years, the prices ranged from ten cents to a low of four cents in 1985. Moreover, those were nominal prices, and the true value was considerably less than it appeared to be. For example, if for comparative purposes we take as a base the depression year of 1932, when sugar declined to three-fourths of a cent, four cents in 1985 was the equivalent of approximately a half cent in real purchasing power. As Marcelo Fernández put it, "Expressed in their real value, the sugar prices [of the 1980s] are comparable with those of the decade of the 1930s . . . that is to say, the lowest prices of the present century" (p. 5). Although prices in the early 1990s showed some improvement, it is evident that Cuba's sugar-dependent economy is on a treadmill; it has to produce more and more sugar just to remain in the same place.

The outlook for the future is not promising. Since the mid-sixties, the trend of world production (cane and beet sugar combined) reveals a gradual increase over world consumption. The average price in the long run could decline rather than improve. Although Cuba remains the leading exporter of cane sugar, it is now second to Brazil in output, while countries like India and Thailand have become significant producers. The European Economic Community's production of sugar (derived from beets) now amounts to nearly twice Cuba's output. At the same time, the use of substitutes such as corn-based fructose, saccharin, and aspertame is increasing. With respect to the critically important capitalist market, Cuban exports have been losing ground both in absolute and in relative terms. Marcelo Fernández calculates (p. 196) that for the five-year period from 1969 through 1973, the average annual amount of sugar exported was nearly 2 million tons. For the five-year period from 1981 through 1985, it was slightly over 1.7 million tons, or a decrease of 15 percent. At the same time, Cuba's share of total sugar imports by capitalist countries also declined, from 13 percent to something under 9 percent. Meanwhile, Cuba's population under the Castro regime has been growing at a faster rate than its output of sugar. Altogether the prospects are dim that either prices or export quantities will rise sufficiently to meet Cuba's growing needs.

Finally, the end of socialism in Eastern Europe, along with German reunification, has meant the end of preferential prices for Cuban sugar in these markets, perhaps the end of the markets themselves, as far as Cuba is concerned. Nor can this outlook be discarded in the case of the crisis-ridden Soviet Union. As for additional sources of hard currency, the current efforts to develop tourism from capitalist countries and to promote the export of citrus and new medical products to capitalist markets, even if successful, can have only marginal importance for years to come. Thus, Cuba for the time being remains saddled with its increasingly unprofitable sugar economy.

How Cuba will disengage from its historic dependency on sugar—as it eventually must—is difficult to foresee. The investment in sugar is enormous and has continued to grow. As of late 1989, some two-thirds of all cultivated land was planted in sugarcane. About four hundred thousand Cubans, with their families representing nearly 15 percent of the total population, were directly involved in producing sugar. Three-quarters were agricultural workers—weeding, fertilizing, and irrigating the cane fields, as well as harvesting and planting new cane. The rest worked in the sugar mills. A likely problem for the future is the role of the state, entrenched in the planning, production, and marketing of sugar since the early sixties. Close to 90 percent is produced on state farms (with 100 percent processed in state-owned sugar mills), the rest by cooperatives and individual small farms, closely regulated by the state. Actually, no other country in the world in modern times has had as high a proportion of its agriculture located in the state sector. In 1985, a census of agrarian property in Cuba revealed that 85 percent belonged to the state, as compared with 65 percent in the Soviet Union, 30 percent in Czechoslovakia, 24 percent in Nicaragua, and 12 percent in Angola.

Between 1980 and 1986, large new investments were made in the sugar sector. Seven new sugar mills were constructed, the first in over fifty years, bringing the total to 160. A major amount of the cost, the equivalent of $643 million, was provided primarily by the Soviet Union, with smaller amounts contributed by the then German Democratic Republic (East Germany) and Bulgaria. Further evidence of the increasing commitment to sugar were wage benefits granted to Cuban sugar workers, who became something like a labor aristocracy. Wages were increased in the early eighties so that mill workers received 230 pesos per month, 35 percent higher than industrial workers in other sectors. The average for field workers was increased to 186 pesos per month, 37 percent higher than wages for other agricultural workers.

In his book, Marcelo Fernández stresses two related developments that took place during the 1980s. One has been the elimination of petroleum as a source of energy for the sugar mills. The substitute source is bagasse, the remains of the cane after grinding. Here the Soviet Union deserves some credit for encouraging Cuban oil conservation and permitting the reexport of any saving on its oil quota. An unexpected result was that for a brief period, petroleum exports edged out sugar as Cuba's leading hard-currency earner. With Soviet oil exports to Cuba now sharply reduced, however, this is not likely to occur again. When I raised this matter with Marcelo Fernández he seemed to agree, but then went on to change the subject: "Neither we nor the Soviets have yet realized the full potentials of social-ism," he said. "And remember that whatever mistakes we Cuban socialists have made, we have produced a much higher level of social services than the country has known in its entire history." I might have suggested that these services were now in danger of drastic deterioration, but I let the matter drop.

The other development emphasized by Fernández has been the exploration of other uses for bagasse, as well as other derivatives or by-products obtained from the sugar production process. At the end of the eighties, ten plants were producing several types of paper, as well as corrugated cardboard and particle board from bagasse, apparently of acceptable quality. However, there has been no success in the critical area of newsprint, all of which has to be import-ed from capitalist sources. In the early nineties, this resulted in a drastic countrywide reduction of newspapers, for the first time in Cuban history. More successful has been the manufacture of torula yeast from a mixture of sugar residue and urea, produced in nearly a dozen plants. The yeast is mixed with molasses (a sugar by-product) to yield a high-protein animal feed. In addition, some factory wastes are now converted into fertilizer. Cuba may well be a world leader in these sugar-derived enterprises.

It is not yet clear to what extent these innovations, laud-able as they are, and the investments they represent can solve the problems of Cuba's sugar-based economy. In the absence of a comprehensive accounting, it is a safe assumption that the development of these new products can have only minor importance. This brings us back to the question of sugar itself. Here, the prospects of increasing productivity and higher output face serious obstacles, as Castro himself admitted in February 1986 in an address to the Third Congress of the Communist party of Cuba: "The growth of sugar production, our most important national industry . . . has been below the possibilities considering the resources invested in it" (p. 179). Castro went on to explain some of the details:

Sugarcane production targets were not met because of insufficient planting and unsatisfactory agricultural yields. Inadequate soil preparation, short supplies of agricultural machinery drawn by high-power tractors, and improper field leveling and drainage resulted in high crop losses. Delays in the development and introduction of new, more productive and disease-resistant varieties, low-quality seeds, ill-timed planting, as well as delays in weeding and cultivation, among other factors, contributed to the low density of many cane fields, which caused limited agricultural yields.

Those are some of the intractable domestic problems of "our most important national industry." And what about the contributions of more than thirty years of socialism and the binding ties with the Soviet Union? Here Castro remains silent. Nor has he ever admitted the decisive importance of his compliance with the Soviet Union, in 1963, to revert to sugar monoculture. It could be said, in his behalf, that at the time his decision appeared rational. On the one hand, the early stages of socialist central planning in Cuba, including the effort to diversify the economy, were extremely discouraging. On the other hand, Cuba had historically been an eminently successful producer and exporter of sugar. Presumably, sugar production and marketing skills were still intact. In addition, sugar would be the logical commodity with which to pay for Soviet imports. The Soviet Union understandably urged Cuba to rely on sugar as a source of demonstrated capacity for paying for Soviet exports and developing its socialist economy. What was unanticipated by both Castro and the Kremlin was that socialism would cripple Cuba's historical expertise in the sugar business.

ONE CAN SPECULATE on what might have happened had Castro's Revolution combined legitimate nationalism and social reform with a largely private-enterprise economy. Often overlooked was the potential for economic progress that existed in Cuba after the elimination of the Batista dictatorship. The Cuban market economy of the fifties was sufficiently mature to provide a base for expansion and modernization. Sufficient Cuban talent existed to promote such an economy. There would have been an accelerated investment of capital by Cuban entrepreneurs, who in the fifties already had developed considerable initiative. As a matter of fact, they then controlled some two-thirds of sugar production. In addition, a policy of properly regulated foreign investment, with access to first-class technology, would have contributed to economic growth, including significant diversification and industrialization. (The example of Taiwan, also a sugar producer, comes to mind.) However, socialism and incorporation within the Soviet bloc created new conditions that effectively inhibited the realization of the earlier potential. Whatever might have been has been forever lost to Castro's Revolution. If Cuba is to regain self-sufficiency and achieve a modern balanced economy, sugar will have to play a different role, and economic forces other than Fidel Castro will have to be in charge.

7 ★ *Out of Africa*

Angola fills me with anguish, not because Neto is a
Communist, not at all—we have good relations with
most of the Communist states—but because Cuba
has interfered in our internal affairs by sending its
army to Africa. . . . And I think that is a very bad
example for Africa, because now when we have argu-
ments or conflicts we will summon the foreigners. I
believe that today our dependence on the foreigner is
more serious than during the time of the colonial
regimes. Under the colonial regime, we could
protest, we had the people with us. Today, we are
colonized and we lie to the people telling them that
they are free.

—Léopold Sédar Senghor, poet and former president
of Sénégal, *Le Monde*, December 26-27, 1976
(my translation)

THE LAST OF CASTRO'S 50,000 TROOPS in Angola returned to Cuba at the end of May 1991. They were greeted with great fanfare as "internationalist heroes." Previously, in early December 1989, the remains of the soldiers who died in Africa, some 2,300, each in a small box, had reached Cuba for reburial. Whether the boxes held cremated ashes or skeletal scraps was not revealed. Some of the soldiers had lost their lives as far back as 1975. The dead were solemnly declared to be "internationalist martyrs." Among them were 160 who fell defending the brutal regime of Mengistu Haile Mariam in Ethiopia and 113 who died in "other sister nations."* The last 3,000 Cuban soldiers, of the original 10,500 in Ethiopia, had been withdrawn in September 1989.

Thus ended an extraordinary chapter in the history of the Cuban Revolution, which is to say, a period in which Fidel Castro adopted a self-appointed role as liberator of oppressed humanity. It was a mission of near Napoleonic dimensions and pretensions. Cuba, a small Caribbean island, in partnership with the Soviet Union, became an African power, supporting proletarian internationalism against South African and American imperialist domination. To further appreciate the magnitude of the Cuban undertaking in Africa, it should be recalled that in Angola alone,

---

* Figures for the dead reported in *Granma Weekly Review,* Dec. 17, 1989.

377,000 Cuban troops were rotated during the fifteen-year period of the war, as well as 50,000 civilians serving as doctors, nurses, teachers, construction workers, administrators, and other specialists.* Cuba, with Soviet assistance, played a dominant role not only in the war but also in the management of key sectors of the economy and public services. Angola took on the appearance of a Cuban colony.

The total number of casualties was not released. If we accept the standard ratio of five injured for each mortality, there probably were nearly 14,000 total casualties in the African campaigns, a significant number for a country of ten million. On a per-capita basis, the equivalent for the United States would have been twenty-five times higher, or some 350,000 casualties, considerably more than the United States suffered in Vietnam. As one scholar pointed out, "Relative to Cuba's population, its troop deployment to Angola [alone] has been larger and has lasted longer than that of the United States to Vietnam at the peak of that war."** There were also other similarities, sometimes overlooked. Both military interventions were in civil wars in distant continents and took place in the context of the cold war. Both claimed to be motivated by lofty principles, although both were in clear violation of the norms of inter-

* *Granma International,* June 2, 1991. This weekly is a much-reduced version of the former *Granma Weekly Review,* discontinued because of paper shortage.
** Domínguez, 18.

national conduct. And both countries failed in their ultimate objectives. The Communists defeated the American
objectives in Vietnam. Despite the Cuban military success
in defending the Communist regime in Angola, the civil
war ended in a military stalemate between the Communists
and their opponents, along with a treaty at the end of May
1991 to form a new Angolan government free of Marxism-
Leninism. As for Ethiopia, the Cuban-backed Communist
government was overthrown in June 1991, signaling the end
of Marxism-Leninism in Ethiopia.

One striking difference between the American and
Cuban experiences was the response of public opinion in
each country. It was largely negative in the United States,
while in Cuba it was mainly positive. A number of factors
contributed to the Cuban attitude. There was no public
debate in Cuba. The intervention in Angola was portrayed
by the tightly controlled media as a noble undertaking to
defend a black Marxist government endangered by racist
South African and imperialist American support of the anti-
Communist faction in the civil war. Cuba's African heritage
was invoked. Cuba's military achievements in a distant land
became a source of national pride. The return of the living
and dead soldiers was skillfully organized into great demon-
strations of patriotism and dedication to true Marxist-
Leninist internationalism.

On my last day in Havana, I had a conversation about
the event with the chambermaid who attended to my room

at the Habana Libre Hotel. She lost two brothers in Angola and was given time off to witness their reburial in Cuban soil. Her eyes filled with tears as she spoke, but she was also proud of her brothers' sacrifice. Her feelings struck me as genuine. Earlier I had talked with a sophisticated Cuban, one who was highly critical of Castro's blind faith in socialism. Yet he had no criticism for Cuban involvement in Angola. He offered the opinion that Cuba's decisive role in defeating the South African forces in southern Angola and, thereby, in securing the independence of Namibia justified the loss of Cuban lives. I silently suspected that national pride affected his judgment. In any event, from all that I could tell, Castro's military adventures in Africa had full popular support and reinforced his image as a true patriot and great leader.

Castro's interest in Africa began shortly after taking power in 1959. For Cubans at the time, except for historians delving into the origins of slavery in Cuba and ethnologists researching African folklore on the island, Africa was a remote continent of no political or economic concern. For Castro, it became an area where anticolonialism offered opportunities for securing political allies in his confrontation with the United States and for promoting his reputation as a champion of the poor and oppressed peoples of the Third World. The first signal of Cuba's new foreign policy orientation occurred in mid-June 1959, when Castro sent Che Guevara on an unprecedented three-month globe-circling tour. It was a demonstration that, for the first time in its history, Cuba had become an independent actor on the international scene, even beyond the confines of the Western Hemisphere. The highlight of the trip was a meeting with President Nasser in Cairo. It revealed Castro's early strategy to identify with the Third World and, in particular, with the recently independent states of Africa.

In September 1960, when Castro attended the Fifteenth General Assembly of the United Nations in New York, his strategy had further crystallized. A formal break with the United States, largely provoked by Castro, was imminent. Cordial relations with the Soviet Union had been established. In his speech before the assembly, he challenged the United States and appealed for support from the Third World. India's Nehru, Egypt's Nasser, and Ghana's Nkrumah, the foremost Third World leaders at the time, responded by ostentatious displays of friendship.

Cuban participation in the First Conference of Heads of State of Nonaligned Countries, held in Belgrade in September 1961, marked another step in consolidating relations with the Third World. Fresh from its stunning victory at the Bay of Pigs, Cuba was the only Latin American country among twenty-five voting delegations, of which eleven were African. Over the years, the Nonaligned Movement became an important arena for Castro in promoting Cuban interests and his personal ambitions. In 1977, Cuba was elected to lead the Nonaligned Movement, and Castro presided over its Sixth Summit Conference held in Havana in September 1979. It was a high point of Cuba's international prestige and a personal triumph for Fidel Castro, despite the obvious paradox that Cuba was in no sense nonaligned.

The direct antecedent of Cuba's major engagement in Angola was Che Guevara's Congo campaign about a decade earlier. That was preceded by Guevara's extended reconnaissance tour, from mid-December 1964 to early March 1965, which included his public appearances in the then seven anti-imperialist countries, among them Ben Bella's Algeria and Nasser's Egypt. There was also a secret excursion into leftist-held territory of the former Belgian Congo (now Zaire), which was to be the scene of Guevara's later military incursion. Among the factors prompting Castro to provide military support to the Marxist-oriented contenders in the Congo civil war was his increasing apprehension about American intentions toward Cuba following the intensification of American military operations against Communist North Vietnam, while both the Soviet Union and China failed to challenge the aggression. Meanwhile, Cuban guerrilla efforts in Latin America had been largely ineffective. Thus a successful counterattack against the American-backed faction in the Congo civil war would provide the much-needed leverage against the United States that had failed to materialize in Latin America.

That objective was unexpectedly revealed by Guevara during his African reconnaissance tour. At one point, he declared that from a military point of view, in Cuba's confrontation with the United States, Africa enjoyed an advantage over Latin America "because of its greater distance from the United States and its greater possibilities for logistical support."* That was a reference to the geographical proximity of anti-imperialist Algeria and Egypt. In Algiers, he told Josephine Fanon, the widow of the renowned Franz Fanon, that "Africa is one, if not the most important, among battlefields against imperialism" (*Revolución* [Havana], December 23, 1964). And again, in an interview in Algiers, he spoke of "combining our resources . . . to resist imperialist aggression, for example, in the Congo" (*Alger Ce Soir*, January 30, 1965). It is important to recall that more than a decade before Cuba's major engagements in Angola and Ethiopia, notwithstanding pious claims of disinterested and high moral purpose, Guevara had confirmed that Cuban involvement in Africa was largely motivated by realpolitik as calculated by Castro in his obsessive confrontation with the United States. Because Castro always equates Cuban interests with his own deeply rooted evangelical aspirations, a personal dimension attached itself to his African undertakings.

In sharp contrast to the later Angolan and Ethiopian campaigns, Guevara's expedition to the Congo, at the head

---

* Cited by Daniel James, *Che Guevara: A Biography* (Chelsea, Mich.: Scarborough House, 1970), 159.

of several hundred Cuban troops, turned out to be a total disaster. Che managed to escape and was not seen in public until his corpse was displayed in a Bolivian jungle village in October 1967. The Congo adventure became a nonevent in Cuban history until early 1977, when Colombian novelist and Nobel Laureate Gabriel García Márquez gave a Castro-approved account of the ongoing Angolan war acknowledging Guevara's earlier campaign. As the document put it, with unintended irony, Guevara's presence in Africa had "planted a seed that no one could uproot."* Despite the disaster in the Congo, Castro continued to meddle discreetly and modestly in African affairs, notably by maintaining contact with the Popular Movement for the Liberation of Angola (MPLA), of Marxist persuasion and favored by the Soviet Union. That set the stage for the major Cuban-Soviet intervention in the civil war that followed when Portugal pulled out of its four-hundred-year colony in early November 1975.

Airlifted Cuban troops arrived just in time to rescue the MPLA, which had seized the capital city, Luanda, and declared itself to be the government of Angola. Then a steady flow of Cuban troops, using newly arrived Soviet military equipment, quickly destroyed an opposing liberation force backed by China and the United States and forced the retreat of a South African incursion. They also managed to

* From extracts published in the *Washington Post*, Jan. 10–12, 1977.

contain another, more durable rival, the National Union for the Total Independence of Angola (UNITA), led by the charismatic Jonas Savimbi, that managed to hold on to about two-thirds of Angolan territory until the settlement of 1991.

An early question raised was whether Cuba or the Soviet Union was the prime mover in their common Angolan engagement. It now appears without question that Castro sent the first Cuban troops without prior consultation with the Soviets. At the same time, it is also clear that Castro was not taking a wild gamble but had reason to expect Soviet approval and military cooperation. García Márquez, in his Cuban-sponsored account, confirmed this in a January 10, 1977, excerpt in the *Washington Post*. "Cuba," he wrote, "was sure it could count on solidarity and material aid from the Soviet Union."

In any event, Cuban troops did not act as a simple surrogate for the Soviet Union, as the Chinese claimed in widely disseminated propaganda. Castro had his own aims concerning the liberation of Angola that, in a sense, he had pursued for more than a decade. They interlocked with Soviet aims. Their joint action in Angola was thus a partnership. At the same time, it must be recognized that Cuba was the junior partner and would have been unable to sustain its military force, beyond its first incursion, without the permission and indispensable logistical support of Moscow. It is also a fact that the Angolan civil war was fundamentally an episode of the cold war in which the Soviet Union was attempting to secure a geopolitical advantage in the former Portuguese colony. Practically speaking ("objectively" in Marxist terminology), Cuba, a small, dependent state heavily subsidized by Moscow, was promoting Soviet long-range geopolitical interests, for it could have no such interests of its own. If it was not, as China claimed, acting as a simple Soviet surrogate, it was in fact, and inevitably, a Soviet auxiliary.

Cuban propaganda to this day stresses the legitimacy of its role in Angola: It had responded to an appeal by the MPLA's self-appointed "government in Luanda," and its response was an exercise of its sovereign right on the international scene. Castro's propaganda has been effective outside Cuba and inside as well. While in Havana in 1989, I raised the question with several generally independent-minded Cubans concerning Cuba's right to intervene in Angolan affairs, and they all accepted the Castro regime's explanation. I suspected that pride over Cuba's military presence on a distant continent made them less sensitive to Castro's violation of the norms of international conduct.

But what about Cuban involvement in Ethiopia? The Cubans I spoke with were less willing to express themselves on that issue. In contrast to the claim of invitation to Angola, Cuba could make no similar claim in the case of Ethiopia, with which it had had no previous involvement, no agenda of its own. In 1977, Cuban troops came to the rescue of the endangered Soviet ally, obviously at Moscow's request. That explains why Cuban propaganda has always underplayed its engagement in Ethiopia. When the celebration of its "internationalist" achievements in Africa were hailed on the return of the living and dead veterans of the Angolan war, mention of Ethiopia was prudently muted.

Just as the cold war had created the conditions for Cuban, Soviet, South African, American and, briefly, Chinese concern with the Angolan civil war, so did the waning and end of the cold war play the determining role in ending hostilities in Angola. Beginning in the mid-eighties, Soviet pressure on Cuba and Angola, and simultaneously American pressure on South Africa, finally led to an agreement to end the war. The terms of the agreement, signed on December 22, 1988, in New York, of all places, included a schedule for the phased total withdrawal of Cuban troops from Angola, an overriding objective of the United States since the arrival of the first Cuban forces. It also recorded the consent of South Africa to grant independence to Namibia. Left for a future date was the uneasy 1991 settlement between the rival Angolan contenders, the MPLA and UNITA, which turned out to be temporary.*

The presence of the Cuban delegation for the first time

---

* As of late September, 1993, "The country seems doomed to months or years more of a lethal standoff that has already created some of the most wretched pockets of misery in Africa and demolished what little remained of the Angolan economy" (*New York Times,* September 24, 1993).

negotiating directly with the United States over an issue of international significance was another feather in Castro's cap. It also confirmed the extent to which Cuba-dominated Angola, presumably a sovereign state, was completely over-shadowed in the final negotiations by its Cuban protector. And those negotiations were, of course, a tribute to Cuban military power, for it had played a decisive role in the survival of the Marxist contenders in the Angolan civil war, just as it previously rescued the Ethiopian Marxist regime at the time of the Somalian invasion.

Yet there are both irony and paradox in Cuba's military achievements. No assessment of Cuban military achievements should overlook Cuban participation in the massive destruction of property and loss of life in Angola and Ethiopia. Many thousands of native combatants and civilians perished. The Angolan economy was completely wrecked, and Ethiopia was reduced to a state of near chaos and starvation. Not only did both Angola and Ethiopia ultimately abandon the Marxism-Leninism that the Cuban military fought to preserve; the withdrawal of Cuban troops from both countries also marked the end of Cuban power in the international arena. With the end of the cold war and the deep transformations in Soviet foreign policy, there was no prospect for any significant Cuban military role beyond its borders.

8 ★ *All that Glitters . . .*

HEN MY WIFE AND I LEFT CUBA in 1968, Roberto Cruz (not his real name) was not quite four years old. When I returned alone in late 1989, he was Dr. Cruz, a physician in Castro's recently established program of family medical services, designed to supplement the traditional Soviet-style polyclinics. He lived with his wife and child in a small apartment above his office and had a roster of 150 neighborhood families as patients. I met him one evening at dinner with his parents, old friends of bygone years. I was fortunate in meeting Roberto, an alert and sophisticated young man, obviously well informed about Cuba's public-health system and uninhibited in his appraisal of its qualities and defects.

One matter that concerned him that evening was the medical bureaucracy and the Communist party that controlled it. He had spent two years in the then German

Democratic Republic specializing in orthopedics. On his return, he expected to be assigned as a specialist in a hospital or polyclinic. Instead, he found himself in a family practice. Nobody questioned his certification as an orthopedic surgeon. The state had invested considerable funds—and he had a huge personal investment—in his training as a specialist, but the "planning" apparatus had a new "plan," and there was no recourse. Roberto had nothing against the family program. He actually thought the idea a good one, but he deplored the arbitrary use of authority and its inefficiency. I also suspected that his motivation toward his work was less than it might have been. His salary as a family physician, among other things, was lower than that of a specialist. I concluded he was in a trap similar to that of most other workers in the socialist system. The state gave him a job but removed the incentive to do more than the minimum required.

Roberto's complaint about bureaucracy reminded me of a urologist I had consulted in Havana in 1963 or thereabouts. He was then in his late fifties. He had been a resident at the Peter Brent Brigham Hospital in Boston and was a United States board certified specialist. Before the Revolution, he had built up a substantial private practice and, at the same time, was on the staff of a large Havana hospital where he served without pay. When I first saw him as a private patient, he had a suite of rooms in a modern medical office building in uptown Vedado. On my next visit, he told me that the building was to be taken over by a ministry (I forget which) and he would have to transfer his private practice to his home. It was a comfortable villa in a pleasant but distant suburb. I was annoyed by the time it took me to drive there on my third and last visit.

I was not the only one annoyed. The doctor was clearly depressed, and before I left, he unburdened himself to me. He had never had any deep interest in politics but was glad to see the end of the Batista dictatorship. He was thus well disposed toward the Revolution and had no thought of leaving Cuba. Now he wondered whether he had made the right decision. He had been told to liquidate his private practice. In addition, he had been asked to "volunteer" to teach anatomy to first-year students at the medical school. The enrollment had tripled, and there was a desperate need for instructors. It was twenty-five years since he had taken his one and only course in anatomy. To teach it now would be a backbreaking task. And what about his years of urological expertise? And who made these decisions? He had lost control of his life and was reduced to the status of serf, "pushed around," as he put it, by incompetent and irrational bureaucrats. It had become intolerable.

"I believe your infection is cured," he told me before I left. "If the problem reoccurs, go to the hospital outpatient clinic. You can't make an appointment. You'll have to wait your turn. I may still be there part-time, but you'll have to take any doctor assigned to you." I never saw him again. I learned that he eventually left Cuba and established a practice as a urologist in Madrid.

In 1959, there were over six thousand physicians in Cuba. About half left the island in the following years. In his speeches Castro often refers to them with scorn as "allies of imperialism" and "traitors" motivated by greed. Chances are that some of them, perhaps many of them, were like my unhappy urologist, prepared to remain in Cuba had they been encouraged to stay and contribute their much-needed skills instead of being "pushed around" unceremoniously. Their mistreatment was costly because it was many years before a new corps of physicians could be created. Castro boasts about overcoming the loss of so many Cuban doctors without acknowledging his contribution to the exodus.

These events and recollections played a role in how I engaged and responded to Roberto Cruz as we talked about Cuba's health-care system. All in all, he considered Castro's public-health policies a success. Whereas there was only one medical faculty at the University of Havana in 1959, a score of medical schools were now functioning across the island, probably more than needed, churning out more doctors than the country could profitably absorb. (Many were "exported" to Africa, the Near East, and Caribbean republics, in some cases earning hard currency that eased the shortage in Cuba.) There were now over twenty thousand doctors (one per 550 inhabitants) and dozens of new hospitals and polyclinics, some in remote rural areas formerly deprived of medical services. Infant mortality rates had been substantially reduced. Inoculation of children against polio and other diseases was universal. Medical research and technology had been improved, to the extent that organ transplants were now performed in Havana. Perhaps the most important achievement was that probably every Cuban had access to basic medical services.

However, Roberto readily acknowledged some flaws. Because of his openness, I asked him to evaluate the credibility of a confidential public opinion poll made by the Communist party in the second half of 1987. It concerned public-health conditions in the province of Holguín, in the northeastern part of the island. It had a mixed urban and rural population of some three hundred thousand (my estimate). The document, entitled *Boletín Especial*, had somehow come into the possession of the anti-Castro Cuban National Foundation of Washington, D.C., which in 1988 published a verbatim copy, accompanied by an English translation. It contained thirty-three pages, excluding several charts at the end. I brought a synopsis of its highlights with me to Cuba in case an opportunity arose to discuss it with a knowledgeable person. Dr. Roberto Cruz turned out to be my man.

The poll revealed an astonishing figure. "From a total of 10,756 opinions," it stated, "87.6 percent are unfavorable. In comparison with the same period of the previous year, there was an increase of 3 percent." Most of the complaints, as summed up in the report, concerned "the lack of attention, negligence and abuse of patients." In the case of the family doctor services, the situation was better, with only "64.9 percent [expressing] unfavorable opinions." Thus, despite "Party and Government efforts and the special attention of Comrade Fidel [Castro] . . . the population is not totally satisfied. . . ."

I cited some random typical complaints to Roberto:

• "When it rains, [the polyclinic] gets flooded."

• "There is a shortage of medications and when they arrive there are very few."

• "When seeing the patients, the doctors do not read their medical histories."

• "Electrocardiogram results are not ready for twelve days."

• "Nurses do not provide good services."

• "The polyclinic has three ambulances but only one driver."

• "For emergency services, at times, one has to wait half a day."

• "When will we have a decent hospital?"

• "Bureaucracy has increased and the attention to patients has decreased."

• "The children are suffering from the heat because there are no fans."

In addition, there were many complaints about the chronic absenteeism of both doctors and nurses and about favoritism in the treatment of well-connected patients.

Roberto listened attentively. He had no knowledge of the particular poll but conceded that the results were credible. He made the point that health services inevitably reflected management and supply problems that plagued most of the socialist enterprises. At the same time, he suggested that the results of the poll should be seen in the perspective of the lack of services, particularly in rural areas, before the Revolution. The complaints reflected expectations that did not exist previously. Nevertheless, he concluded, there was still a long way to go despite the enormous investment in public health of the last thirty years.

Later, the Holguín public opinion poll reminded me of another Communist Party survey of some years ago. Originally confidential, it was unexpectedly published in the daily *Granma* on November 28, 1967. It dealt with living conditions in El Purio, a small provincial settlement and its surrounding rural area in the central part of the island. At the time, Castro was extolling the extraordinary benefits that the Revolution had brought to the Cuban countryside. Like the contrast between the official public-health pronouncements and the gross inadequacies revealed by the Holguín poll, there was a remarkable discrepancy between Castro's claims and reality, for the conclusions of the El Purio investigation were entirely negative. In fact, conditions were shocking: "The inhabitants . . . lack a sense of community and stability. . . . There were two television sets, neither of which was functioning. There was a lack of any kind of cultural or sport facilities. . . . The town received no books or magazines. Distribution of necessities was irregular. . . . *There were difficulties in taking children to a doctor* [situated in another town]. . . . *There was no pharmacy* [my emphasis and translation]."

Very likely, in the years that followed, some changes for the better had taken place, but given the perennial problems of Cuba's socialist economy and bureaucratic mismanagement, the suspicion lingers that El Purio remains an isolated and retarded community.

As Roberto and I discussed the Holguín poll, he revealed another obstacle to better health services. Cubans had developed a tendency to seek medical advice about trivial and suspected ailments that increased the work load and irritability of doctors and nurses. Patients paid no fees. They had little instruction concerning self-medication of minor discomforts, such as headaches and colds. Instead of taking aspirin or drinking lots of fluids, they would first clog the waiting rooms to see a doctor. Here Roberto made a special point: There was a heavy investment in treatment facilities and very little in providing the public with health information.

Turning to another topic, I expressed some skepticism concerning the highly publicized low rate of infant mortality. According to Cuban statistics, accepted by the World Health Organization (WHO), approximately only ten infants per thousand live births died before completing their first year. That was not far out of line with the infant mortality rate of highly industrialized countries, with the exception of Japan, where the rate was only five per thousand. The rate in countries like Mexico, Peru, and Brazil was considerably higher; but in Costa Rica and Barbados, countries often considered relatively primitive in their health care facilities and systems, the rate was only marginally higher than it was in Cuba. (Apparently, Castro's socialism is not the determining factor.)

Roberto agreed that Cuban statistics were not entirely reliable, and he expressed surprise about the WHO data showing Costa Rica and Barbados on a par with Cuba. Since no other source of information was available, there was no choice but to accept the WHO data. In any event, he was convinced that in Cuba there had been considerable improvement in recent years. This, he said, reflected not only the greater availability of professional obstetrical and newborn services in Cuba but also the assimilation of advances in medical technology in the world at large. At the same time, he was critical of deficiencies in prenatal care leading to low birth weights and premature birth. (This problem, it should be noted, is not restricted to Cuba. It is a matter of concern as well in the United States and other industrial countries.) Too many pregnant Cuban women smoked and consumed alcoholic beverages. Too few consulted doctors early in pregnancy. It was largely, he said, the result of too little health education. Infants with low birth weights tend to be at increased risk of physical problems such as lung disorders. They are also apt to suffer from emotional or learning disabilities and to face a lifetime of poor health.

There were other matters related to public health that I could have discussed with Roberto, but time did not permit. One question I had wanted to raise was about the effectiveness of family-planning facilities that were established in Cuba a number of years earlier. Given the regime's acceptance of birth control, no one publicly opposes the distribution of contraceptive devices. Likewise, there are few restrictions on abortions, which are performed free of charge in hospitals and clinics. There is no right-to-life movement in Cuba. Consequently, one might have imagined considerable success in the prevention of unwanted pregnancies, certainly in comparison with the record in the United States.

It thus came as a surprise to discover, according to a report in the former *Granma Weekly Review* of May 14, 1989, that "one of the greatest social problems in Cuba is teenage pregnancy, which is linked to higher rates of . . . maternal mortality and a large number of adolescents who drop out of school to raise their babies or go to work." The report adds that "sex education is included in [the] school curriculum, but few teachers have been properly trained to impart this material." In addition, a cultural factor is cited for one of the reasons for teenage pregnancies. The condom is rejected "outright" by "most Cubans—both men and women. . . . 'They diminish pleasure,' commented a 30 year old woman who considers condom a dirty word."

For whatever reasons, the persistence of teenage pregnancies—"one of the greatest social problems in Cuba"—represents a conspicuous failure of Castro's public-health program. One goal of Cuban socialism was to eliminate this scourge of capitalist society. As a postscript to this topic, it should be noted that the intensification of Cuba's economic crisis in the early nineties has further complicated problems of sexual behavior and hygiene. A correspondent of Toronto's *Globe and Mail* reported from Havana (April 17, 1991) that "supplies of Kohinoor, the Cuban brand of condoms, are hard to come by." Those complaining include the increasing number of Cuban women, including university students, involved in prostitution, allegedly all but wiped out by the Revolution. They seek out tourists as a way to obtain the hard currency needed to shop in special stores carrying an abundance of imported goods. One "respectable" prostitute was quoted as saying, "We have to get food on the table somehow; there's no way to survive otherwise. I believe in Communism, but I'm not prepared to die for it."

Comprehensive public-health services, comparable in many respects to those of Cuba, exist in many countries (with the notable exception of the United States). Cuba, however, is unique in its management of the acquired immunodeficiency syndrome (AIDS). Since 1986, Cuba has been the only country to require compulsory human immunodeficiency virus (HIV) testing of all its citizens. All carriers, that is, those with positive reactions, are placed in involuntary and lifetime isolation in special sanitariums popularly known as *sidatorios*, a term derived from the Spanish acronym SIDA corresponding to AIDS. Patients actually sick with AIDS are hospitalized elsewhere. The drastic quarantine system has raised questions in the international community concerning its medical effectiveness and its obvious human rights violations.

A variety of international news sources, including Cuban journals, have charted the Cuban government's peculiar method of dealing with AIDS. The Cubans established their first sanitarium on the outskirts of Havana in April 1986, with twenty-four internees. Castro's optimism about the program—"While the world AIDS rate climbs, in Cuba, it is declining" (*Granma Weekly Review,* January 28, 1990)—was not confirmed. Three additional facilities had to be created, two in the center of the island and one at the eastern end. By the end of 1990, a total of more than five hundred HIV-positive Cubans "had been banished for life" (*Globe and Mail,* April 17, 1991). At the same time, new admissions were delayed for lack of space.

Living conditions for the inmates have been described as acceptable or sometimes better, judged by current Cuban standards. Two or three times a year, inmates are permitted to leave the detention grounds, always accompanied by chaperones. Nevertheless, attempts to escape are not uncommon, and are sometimes successful. One inmate, interviewed in the official press, is reported to have said, "There are days when you get depressed and want to leave," a rare admission to appear in print. However, it was modified by his patriotic acceptance of his plight when he added, "But you realize internment is necessary to protect society" (*Granma Weekly Review*, December 10, 1989). Even so, the more common response of such an inmate to a foreign questioner, always in the presence of an official guide, is that he is doing his duty "to defend the Revolution." Following a visit to Havana for a firsthand look at Cuba's "war on AIDS," two open-minded Columbia University hematologists (identified as R. Bayer and C. Healton) concluded in a letter to the *New York Times* (January 22, 1989), "As visitors to their sanitarium, we came away with heavy hearts and minds full of contradictory feelings."

It is well known that AIDS cannot be spread through casual contact, as is the case, for example, with active tuberculosis where the isolation of an infected person could be justified. What, therefore, prompted the Castro regime to require permanent quarantine for HIV carriers who are otherwise healthy and able to carry on a normal life for an indefinite period (the median latency from infection to clinical AIDS being calculated at ten years)? I suggest several related explanations:

• Cuba suffers from the same irrational fears and prejudices experienced in other countries where, however, education and in some cases court action have been used to prevent abuses.

• Castro's regime is concerned about the many thousands of Cuban soldiers and civilians returning from AIDS-infected regions of Africa, as well as the increase in Cuba of venereal diseases such as syphilis and gonorrhea.*

• In contrast to virtually every other nation, Cuba rejected education as the central or dominant element in its anti-AIDS strategy. As the two experts from the Columbia University School of Public Health reported on their return from Cuba, "Education was considered unreliable as a means of modifying behavior—either in infected persons, who posed a threat, or uninfected persons, who might otherwise learn to protect themselves" (p. 1024). In my visit at the end of 1989, I found this attitude prevalent among otherwise dissident Cubans, who cited Cuba's macho sexual traditions as the reason. At the same time, they also revealed a lamentable insensitivity to the issue of individual human rights.

• Cuba's extended public-health organization, combined

---

* According to Cuban statistics cited in R. Bayer and C. Healton, "Controlling AIDS in Cuba: The Logic of Quarantine," *New England Journal of Medicine* 15 (1989): 1022–24. Subsequent page citations in text are to this source.

with the state's power of enforcement, provided a ready-made mechanism for implementing the program.

• For more than thirty years, Cubans have been indoctrinated with the premise that the rights of society, as determined by the state, take precedence over those of the individual.

• Finally, the importance of the issue and the manner of dealing with it undoubtedly reflect the decisive input of Fidel Castro in the adoption of Cuba's unique AIDS program. He had a golden opportunity to prove again his devotion to the common welfare and at the same time demonstrate his capacity to implement a solution on a grand scale unmatched anywhere else in either the socialist or the capitalist world.

What about the effectiveness of the Cuban model? The Columbia University public-health specialists cited above were of the opinion that it could "radically alter the threat of an epidemic. It is doubtful, however," they added, "whether such a system can halt the spread of infection entirely, since . . . some persons will become infected . . . after testing and go on to infect others." As a consequence, they concluded, "it will be necessary to test all Cubans . . . repeatedly and often" (p. 1024). They also pointed out that, given prevailing laboratory standards, it is "inevitable that some false positive results will be generated, and in Cuba the consequence—quarantine—is grave" (p. 1023). They noted that "the Cuban authorities with whom we spoke were concerned over the possibility of both false positive and false negative findings" (p. 1023). In a concluding statement, they reminded the reader that "the imperatives of prevention, however important, are not the only values to be considered in the struggle against AIDS" (p. 1024).

Finally, there is a question of the financial costs of the Cuban model. Castro's government has released no figures, but it is a safe assumption that the screening is expensive. In the United States, a number of calculations have been made in connection with possible insurance benefits for employers. The consensus reached was that "AIDS testing doesn't pay," according to Peter Passell writing in the *New York Times* (July 3, 1991). From a "low risk population pool," he reports, "it is estimated that the typical cost of identifying one HIV-positive . . . would exceed $300,000." While not entirely relevant to Cuba, the calculation suggests a sizable economic burden in Cuba's case. To this must be added the costs of building and maintaining Cuba's detention facilities.

This brings up an important, indeed decisive, point concerning Cuba's entire public-health system. Castro himself has referred to it on at least two occasions that I know of, in both instances in connection with appeals for improvement in work standards. "Our educational and medical services are way above what our material economic base allows us," he stated in a speech reported in *Granma Weekly Review*, May 2, 1971. "Our expenses in education

and public health are above our resources and possibilities."
Then in another speech on December 2, 1986 (*Granma
Weekly Review*, December 14, 1986), he elaborated on the
same theme: "Speaking absolutely frankly, the luxury we
have had in our country . . . [with] education, health care
and decent standards of living is made possible not by our
work, but by what we have received through internationalism," the familiar code word for the Soviet Union.

Thus, Cuba's costly and frequently admired public-
health services have been made possible only by the generous subsidies of the Soviet Union. With the phasing out of
these subsidies by the end of 1991, the services are being
sharply reduced, including the Castro-inspired AIDS prevention program, which may have to be entirely abandoned.
"And what about the future?" I asked Roberto. "I suspect
that with diminishing imports from the Soviet Union and
Eastern Europe, shortages will get worse and medical supplies will be difficult to obtain." Roberto was deeply pes-
simistic. He remarked that nutritional problems were
already evident. He thought that people were still getting
enough calories but insufficient vitamins and minerals. He
had just learned that aspirin was about to be rationed, and
he feared that in time it would be practically unobtainable.
Hospitals built for air-conditioning, and thus windowless,
were facing major problems. With the growing shortage of
electricity, there would be no choice but to break down
walls to permit fresh-air ventilation. His final comment on

the matter expressed the worry that with the breakdown of public transportation, hospital personnel, including indispensable surgeons and nurses, would find it impossible to maintain normal schedules, and general health care would necessarily deteriorate.

Roberto's bleak picture was prophetic. According to information I have received from a later medical visitor to Cuba, further deterioration has been severe. And that information has been confirmed, as a kind of postscript to Roberto's sad comments, in a recent *New York Times* article (April 25, 1993): "Early this month the Cuban Health Ministry announced that there was an epidemic of blinding eye disease caused, in part, by the lack of Vitamin B in the daily Cuban diet."

9 ★ "The Cleanest Trial in History"

A FEW MONTHS BEFORE MY ARRIVAL in 1989, Cuba had been rocked by the most thunderous scandal and trial of the regime's tenure. Yet during my visit shortly after the trial, I was stunned to find that the whole event had been absorbed and apparently forgotten by the Cuban people—an extraordinary illustration of Fidel Castro's power of personality and his ability to manipulate the people of Cuba. Nowhere but in Cuba could a regime suffer such a scandal in the full light of a public trial and survive.

From mid-June to mid-July 1989, with full radio, television, and press coverage, Havana entertained the Cuban people and the whole world with a spectacular trial. It concerned corruption and drug trafficking at the highest military and security levels. The proceedings were closed to the public. Instead, edited videotapes were broadcast in frequent installments and transcribed in the daily *Granma*. Because of the editing, we may never learn in full what transpired, but enough was released to expose a host of skeletons in the closets of the Cuban Revolution. After the close of the trial, all the testimony carried by *Granma*, with additional tables, graphs, and photos, was reprinted in a 480-page book with the exhilarating title of *Vindicación de Cuba*, in an edition of 150,000 copies. It was to be followed by versions in English, French, Portuguese, and Russian. It was a publishing event without precedent, emphasizing the urgency of refurbishing the reputation of the Cuban Revolution and, in particular, its Maximum Leader. For some, at least, it suggested that Fidel Castro "doth protest too much."

As a result of the trial, fourteen high-ranking army and security officers were convicted of treason and corruption. Four, including highly decorated General Arnaldo Ochoa, one-time commander of fifty thousand Cuban troops in Angola, were executed. Ten were sent to prison for up to thirty years. Long prison terms are normal in Castro's Cuba, but executions have been infrequent since the settling of accounts with Batista "war criminals" in 1959, the year Castro took power. It was a special kind of treason of which General Ochoa and his co-defendants were guilty. As defined by the prosecution, *treason* was the act of betraying the high moral standards of the Cuban Revolution. That ultimate offense occurred when the defendants collaborated with the Colombian drug trafficking cartel headed by the notorious Pablo Escobar. As a result, Cuba lost its moral authority, the country's most important "defensive weapon."

The betrayal was even more serious because Fidel Castro, on various occasions, denied charges leveled by the United States that Cuba was engaged in drug trafficking. Hence, the convicted Cuban officials had undermined the credibility and called into question the honor of Fidel Castro, Cuba's supreme leader and paragon of Communist virtue. In addition, their participation in the smuggling of narcotics into the United States amounted to a "hostile act against a foreign state," which could provoke retaliation in the form of armed attack. Outside Cuba, few could accept that argument seriously. In Washington it had been long estimated that an invasion of Cuba would cost fifty thousand American casualties. But Castro had used this polemic before and had need of it again.

As for *corruption*, it had its usual meaning of misuse of official position for personal gain (including black-market speculation) and for high living (wine, women, and song). In a country with a long history of scarcity of material goods, like Cuba, that kind of corruption was endemic, socialist ethics notwithstanding. During the three decades of Castro's socialism, there had been a number of campaigns to eliminate corruption from the higher echelons of the bureaucracy. This time, corruption was more conspicuous. The defendants were handsomely rewarded by the Colombian cocaine smugglers, and a number flaunted their new cars and other expensive gadgets. In addition, the meaning of corruption was broadened to include a predilection for private business deals favored by some of the defendants, most notably General Ochoa. In the context of that 1989 trial, *business* conjured up not the tired images of fat Western democracies but the pictures of Gorbachev's evil perestroika.

Making matters worse for the defendants, and turning up the heat under Castro as well, was the unfortunate timing of these matters of treason and corruption. The dereliction occurred in a special period of what Castro defined as "Rectification of Errors and Struggle Against Negative Tendencies." He initiated the process in 1986, in connection with his rejection of perestroika and glasnost. Thus, three years after the inauguration of the all-out campaign to purify Cuban socialism, and thirty years after creating socialism in Cuba, this worst corruption scandal since Castro came to power was a major embarrassment.

In the aftermath of the trial, two members of Castro's cabinet were sacked, one of whom, José Abrantes, the minister of the interior, was given a twenty-year sentence in a separate trial. (Abrantes died in prison in early 1991, reportedly of a heart attack.) In addition, scores of officials in various ministries were demoted or dismissed. It was easily the biggest purge in thirty years. The trial was also noteworthy in that practically all the defendants had been in service for twenty years or more, had excellent or even distinguished records, and were completely loyal to the Castro regime. As the prosecution admitted, nothing remotely related to counterrevolutionary activity, or even political dissent, was involved in the trial (although it was said that corruption often led to crossing the line).

In the spring of 1964, on the occasion of the earlier trial of Marcos Rodríguez, also a dramatic spectacle, Fidel spoke of the mythological Saturn, the Roman god who devoured his children. He pledged that the Cuban Revolution would never devour its own children. Twenty-five years later, an aging and deeply frustrated Castro broke his pledge. The action added to the feverish speculation concerning Castro's survival. There was widespread belief abroad that the loyalty of the armed forces had been shaken. The *New York Times* (June 25, 1989) reported that in Cuba the sanity of Castro was said to be questioned. Wayne Smith, a seasoned and sober observer of the Cuban scene, happened to be in Havana while the trial was under way. "This case has really stunned Cuba," he was reported to have said. "Wherever you go, people on the street are shocked and talking about it and questioning the official explanation."

Yet, in Havana just six months later, I was surprised to discover that the whole episode seemed to have been forgotten. When I brought the matter up with an old and experienced friend, he dismissed it as one of Castro's recurring tantrums, albeit the most spectacular in memory. Yet in his view, despite the large number of prominent victims, Castro emerged with no loss of power or prestige. On the contrary, Castro had effectively demonstrated that he remained in full control of the state and of public opinion. It became clear to me that whatever Castro's aims in mounting the extraordinary theatrical performance, he had been successful, once more proving his skills as producer and director of political drama, as well as its leading actor.

The play opened with an announcement in *Granma*, on June 14, 1989, that General Arnaldo Ochoa was arrested and would go to trial, charged with "serious deeds of corruption." Despite his previous merits, "the party and Revolutionary Armed Forces cannot in the slightest degree accept the impunity of those . . . who commit serious violations of socialist morality and laws" (*Vindicación*, p. 1). The fifty-seven-year-old Ochoa was not an ordinary general. He was a veteran of the guerrilla war in the Sierra Maestra, later trained in the top military academy of the Soviet Union. He had participated in a covert infiltration in Venezuela. He was commander of troops in Ethiopia, military advisor of the Sandinista government in Nicaragua, commander in chief of the Cuban forces in Angola, member of the Central Committee of the Communist party of Cuba, a deputy of the National Assembly, and officially decorated as a hero of the Republic of Cuba. No one of his stature had ever before been charged with committing any crime. It appeared that an extraordinary event in the Cuban Revolution was about to take place.

There followed what might be called the prologue to the drama in the form of two editorials in *Granma*. The first, on

June 16, declared that Ochoa would be brought before a military Honor Tribunal, according to army regulations. It then made the startling revelation that, in addition to his criminal black-market operations and misuse of funds in Angola, he had engaged in a "much more serious [crime], without precedent in the history of the Cuban Revolution: Ochoa, along with functionaries of the Ministry of the Interior, contacted international drug traffickers, reached an agreement with them and . . . cooperated in drug trafficking operations close to our territory." The reference was to Cuban-controlled coastal waters where, in one transfer variation, planes coming from Colombia dropped waterproof bundles of drugs, which were then recovered by speedboats from Miami.

That was especially reprehensible because "it may have provided a basis for the insidious campaigns of imperialism against the Cuban Revolution" (i.e., American charges that the Cuban government engaged in drug trafficking). The arrest of others implicated in the drug smuggling was also announced, including army captain Jorge Martínez (aide to General Ochoa), Colonel Antonio de la Guardia, and Major Amado Padrón of the Ministry of the Interior (in charge of security), the three who, along with Ochoa, were ultimately executed (*Vindicación*, pp. 2-6).

The second part of the prologue, a voluminous *Granma* editorial of June 22, 1989 (*Vindicación*, pp. 8-21), laid out the drug trafficking charges in detail. It alleged that Ochoa began to take an interest in the drug trade in mid-1986, during a period when he was assigned to duties in Cuba. His aide, Captain Martínez, on his return from a trip to Panama (where the then ruler, General Manuel Antonio Noriega, gave shelter to dummy Cuban corporations), reported to Ochoa that he had been in contact with an Italian-American smuggler who proposed Cuban cooperation in laundering illegal drug money. Ochoa approved the proposition, though apparently nothing came of it. On a subsequent trip to Panama in late 1986, Martínez met a Colombian working for Pablo Escobar, leader of the so-called Medellín drug cartel, a powerful figure in the international drug trafficking business.

The meeting led to Ochoa's decision that Martínez should rendezvous with the drug chief in Colombia. In time, Martínez received a false Colombian passport in Panama from Escobar's agent and finally, in May 1988, traveled via Panama to Medellín where he met with Escobar. He reached an agreement that Cuba would be used as a protected staging area for the transfer of cocaine to speedboats coming from Miami. By that time, Ochoa had gone to Angola to take command of the Cuban troops. He had also discovered that Colonel Tony de la Guardia was already dealing with the Colombian drug cartel. They began to cooperate, with Martínez shuttling back and forth from Angola to Cuba as Ochoa's representative. However, de la Guardia, who controlled a critically important unit of the

Ministry of the Interior, emerged as the key figure in the operation, leaving the disgruntled Ochoa only marginally involved.

For the first time, the editorial revealed that there existed in the Ministry of the Interior a top secret department engaged in smuggling American goods to Cuba. Presumably, the activity began in the sixties after the United States had instituted an embargo on trade with Cuba. When de la Guardia took charge in 1982, the smuggling apparatus was called Department Z. Soon after, the name was changed to Department MC and under that name became the center of Cuban drug trafficking. As described in *Granma*, MC "acquired and transported to Cuba . . . anything that could be useful to our country, absolutely just and moral activities in the face of the criminal blockade of the United States" (*Vindicación*, p. 14). Its functions required it to be exempt from the normal controls of the Cuban border immigration and aeronautical authorities. MC admittedly had connections in the United States with criminal elements experienced in illegal business transactions that could include the import and distribution of drugs. To be sure, the words *smuggling* and *smugglers* in relation to the activities of MC do not appear in the text. At the same time, it was explained that MC was "forbidden to have any connections with elements involved in one way or another with drugs" (*Vindicación*, p. 15). Whether the explicit prohibition was a recent invention cannot be verified. In any event, it appeared important to attribute a patriotic and moral purpose in the creation of MC because it was obvious that it engaged in shady deals with underworld elements and that its existence was decisive in providing the mechanism for Cuban participation in supplying narcotics to the United States.

The editorial calculated that MC, with Ochoa's complicity, facilitated the transfer to the United States of approximately six tons of Colombian cocaine, for which its operatives received commissions amounting to some $3,400,000. The defendants claimed to have turned over most of this sum to the state as part of normal commercial transactions. However, about $1,000,000 was discovered in their possession when they were arrested. Presumably, the rest had been remitted to the state. It was also revealed that Ochoa had a secret bank account of $200,000 in Panama, the proceeds of black-market operations in Angola (*Vindicación*, pp. 18, 19).

Considerable attention in the editorial was focused on exactly how Cuban authorities discovered the drug violations. "It is *very important*" (my emphasis), it declared, "to point out that when Ochoa was arrested on June 12, there was no information at all concerning activities related to drug trafficking. The investigation was concerned with illegal business transactions, corruption, immorality [presumably too indecent for print] and other irregularities of Ochoa in which it appeared that Tony de la Guardia . . . was closely involved. A few hours after the arrest, documents were found [in one house] that raised serious suspicions concerning [drugs]." The point apparently was made to emphasize the claim not only that the drug trade was unauthorized by the government (i.e., by Fidel Castro or his brother, Raúl, minister of the armed forces) but also that the discovery was a sheer accident (*Vindicación*, pp. 16, 17). Defending the innocence of the Castro brothers, in particular Fidel, turned out to have special importance throughout the proceedings.

Finally, the importance and the authority of the editorial were made clear by the last paragraph: "*Granma* not only expresses its editorial opinion but also the opinion of the Central Committee of our party, the commander in chief [Fidel Castro], the Revolutionary Armed Forces [Raúl Castro] and the Ministry of the Interior" (*Vindicación*, p. 21). For Cubans, the solemn invocation of the authority of the highest levels of the State left no doubt that the editorial was, in fact, a guilty verdict against the defendants. What was not yet revealed was the punishment they were to receive.

The trial proper was staged in three parts, as if it were a play in three acts. The first took place on June 25-26. It was a session of the so-called Honor Tribunal that, according to military regulations, was called upon to sit in judgment of an officer with the rank of general. In the Ochoa hearing, it consisted of his peers in the armed forces and included forty-six generals and one admiral. Among the generals was

Fidel Castro's brother, Raúl, Cuba's highest-ranking general and minister of the armed forces, and thus Ochoa's immediate superior. In his testimony, Raúl spoke of his long and intimate friendship with Ochoa and his family, of Ochoa's brilliant record, but also of more recent and troubling symptoms of declining interest in his duties. His attraction toward private business activities aroused suspicion. In short, it was a developing weakness of character and in no sense a lack of discipline or high moral purpose in the armed forces or its leadership that converted a hero of the Republic to a traitor. Raúl suggested that Ochoa's past merits, "far from mitigating his guilt, should increase the severity of his punishment for having betrayed the honor and confidence placed in him" (*Vindicación*, p. 35).

None of those who testified expressed any doubt that Ochoa betrayed his country. As for the defendant, his testimony was brief. He admitted that all the charges leveled at him were true; therefore, he saw no reason to discuss them. "I betrayed my country," he confessed. "Treason is punished with death." He ended with a dramatic declaration: Should he face an execution squad, "I promise all of you that my last thought will be for Fidel, for the great Revolution which he has given our people. Thank you" (*Vindicación*, p. 42). It would seem that Ochoa, knowing how the Cuban system of justice worked, had decided that any attempt to defend himself would be futile. His best hope for clemency was to make a clean breast of it and reassert eternal loyalty to Fidel. It turned out to be a miscalculation.

The verdict was unanimous, and there was no clemency. It recommended that Ochoa (1) be stripped of all his honors, decorations, and medals; (2) be deprived of his rank as general and be dishonorably discharged from the army; (3) be expelled from the Communist party and its Central Committee, as well as the National Assembly, where he served as a deputy; and (4) be brought before a special court-martial to face charges of high treason against his country. In a lengthy commentary explaining and justifying the verdict, published in *Granma* on July 3, a significant statement appeared: "It is evident that U.S. intelligence knew by the first semester of 1987 that planes from Colombia transporting drugs were landing in Varadero with the complicity of Cuban officials." Varadero, on the north coast facing Florida, is Cuba's main tourist center. One method used by the Colombian drug smugglers was to store their cargo in Varadero, from where it was transferred at intervals to Miami-bound speedboats.

U.S. intelligence "knew who these [Cuban] officials were, because as we are now aware it had infiltrated agents among the traffickers." Nevertheless, "it did not communicate a single word, officially or confidentially, to the Cuban government. No doubt they were compiling information and preparing to release incontrovertible evidence" proving Cuban complicity in drug trafficking. The Cuban government believed they had now anticipated and "completely destroyed" their plot (*Vindicación*, pp. 50, 51).

This raises a question about the explanation given concerning the timing of the trial. Was it purely an "accident," as claimed, or rather a preemptive move to nullify an anticipated offensive by American propaganda? In considering this question, it should be recalled that on a number of occasions going back to the early 1980s, the U.S. Drug Enforcement Agency, the State Department, and grand juries in Miami had publicly charged Cuba with participating in drug trafficking. Notably on November 15, 1982, a court in Miami had convicted in absentia four high-ranking Cuban officials on charges of complicity in smuggling narcotics into the United States. Cuban motivation was said to be a reciprocal arrangement by which the Colombian drug merchants would smuggle Cuban weapons to leftist guerrillas in Colombia. In addition, Fidel Castro was mentioned in the indictment of General Noriega, the Panamanian leader, returned by a federal grand jury in Miami in February 1988. It claimed that Castro met with Noriega in Havana "on or about June 29, 1984." The purpose of the meeting was to arrange for Castro to mediate a dispute between Noriega and members of the Medellín cartel about the cartel's cocaine operations in Panama.

However, most of the evidence came from convicted drug runners, who may have been cooperating with the American authorities in return for reduced sentences. Hence, the evidence could be considered tainted. As a result, the Cuban authorities, and Castro personally, could feel they were on safe ground when they indignantly rejected the drug charges as part of the relentless campaign of slander against the Cuban Revolution. Now, in the spring of 1989, Cuba, which is to say Fidel Castro, was convinced that there was evidence that could not be denied. Whatever else may have entered into the decision to hold a spectacular show trial, it is safe to assume that a main purpose was to surprise the Americans with a preemptive acknowledgment of the facts.

THE COURT MARTIAL, or Act 2 of the drama, began on June 30. There were now fourteen defendants, including Ochoa. The text of the proceedings covered some 250 pages, or more than half of *Vindicación de Cuba*. However, most of the crucial evidence had already been presented in what I described as the prologue, and the verdicts were foregone conclusions. Thus, I shall limit my review to only a few additional details.

Unlike his conduct before the Honor Tribunal, the now thoroughly disgraced Ochoa, stripped of all his titles as well as his military uniform, made some effort to defend himself. He was probably convinced that, instead of the clemency he had hoped for, he now faced the death penalty. Thus, he tried to persuade the court that his intentions were honorable. His smuggling of diamonds and ivory from Angola was intended to raise funds to improve the living conditions of the troops under his command. Another private project was to build a much-needed military airport in southwestern Angola. The money in his Panamanian bank account was earmarked to procure vehicles for the army. His income from drug trafficking was to be invested through a go-between in a joint enterprise with the Cuban government to promote the tourist industry in Cuba, currently the country's top economic priority, and so on (*Vindicación*, p. 71). But those intentions were dismissed by the prosecution as fabrications or delusions. To what extent they were either or both cannot be determined because in the Cuban system of justice, there are no restraints on the prosecution. It cannot be challenged by cross-examination, and the function of the defendant's court-appointed lawyers is merely to ask for clemency. However, from Ochoa's admissions, greed was hard to eliminate as part of his motivations.

Apart from Ochoa's case, one of the striking impressions provided by the many hours of testimony was the spectacle of pervasive corruption in the Cuban armed forces. Cuban sugar, flour, and salt, among other commodities, were sold in the ubiquitous *candogas* (black markets) of Luanda, and Angolan currency was illegally traded for American dollars. Wholesale quantities of radios for the troops were purchased by officers who received generous kickbacks. Weapons that were to go to Nicaragua never arrived, and the payment in dollars ended up in private Cuban accounts in Panama. Then there was the matter of "immorality," an obvious reference to sexual debauchery, so shocking it could not be printed. One episode did come to light. It was the case of a young Cuban woman who, in February 1988, disguised in a military uniform, was smuggled into Angola. She remained a month and then was smuggled back to Cuba (*Vindicación*, p. 430).

Two points were constantly stressed at the court-martial and, indeed, throughout the trial. One was the repeated testimony elicited from the defendants that neither Fidel nor Raúl had any knowledge of the drug trafficking. Only one low-ranking defendant, a female officer, had the temerity to testify that she "had heard colleagues . . . saying that their operations were known at the highest levels in Cuba." The other point was the outrageous betrayal of Fidel Castro, who time and again had denied Cuban complicity in the drug traffic. Fidel is a "symbol," the prosecutor declared, "an historic example of honesty never clouded by a lie. . . . Fidel is our voice . . . our representative, to whom we turn in difficult times. . . . He enjoys the authority of public opinion, foreign governments and international agencies when it comes to clarifying the real situation in our country in all spheres and the most delicate times" (*Vindicación*, p. 298). In another country and at another time, that kind of supreme virtue and wisdom would be associated with the cult of personality.

Act 3, the concluding part of the drama, took place on July 9. It was a session of the State Council that consisted of twenty-nine members of the top leadership of the government and Communist party, with Fidel Castro as chairman. According to regulations, in the case of a death sentence imposed by a court-martial, the State Council is required either to confirm the sentence or to commute it to thirty years in prison. The State Council, as expected, unanimously approved the death sentences. Ochoa and the other three condemned men were executed by a firing squad at dawn on July 13.

As could be anticipated, the star performer at the State Council session was Fidel Castro, who spoke at great length with his customary skill and authority. He reviewed the entire case against the accused and in the course of his exposition revealed that he had personally ordered and managed the investigation and orchestrated the trial. That was no surprise to anybody familiar with his habits and talents, though this time he appeared to be unusually sensitive about his role, insisting that he did not impose any decisions. Yet there was one surprise. In accounting for the delay in discovering Cuban complicity in drug trafficking, he essentially repeated what had already been stated earlier in the trial, except for one revelation. It was an indirect reply to a question in many minds but never raised or even hinted at during the trial: How could Fidel Castro *not* have known about so conspicuous and dangerous a dereliction within the ranks of the Ministry of the Interior and in the high command of the armed forces, the guardians of the security and honor of the Revolution? Castro's explanation was that he was totally preoccupied with the war in Angola, which had reached a critical point. "Under what circumstances did the events leading up to the trial take place?" he asked. "They took place while a war raged on. . . . Our country staked everything by sending its best weapons and over 50,000 men there." As a result, he continued, he "received instant news of every man wounded in combat . . . or of those who were killed. . . . We felt responsible for the lives of each and every one . . . all 50,000 of them, and we practically didn't do government work in 1988." At another point, he repeated that from "mid-November 1987 to late 1988, we didn't do government work; we dedicated all our time, all of it, to that struggle, to that war. . . . . I spent 80 percent of my time on this battle. We put aside key things in view of the serious situation that had developed" (*Vindicación*, p. 408).

Then, to prove his complete dedication to the fighting in Angola, he read from hitherto secret messages he had sent to the battlefront. Here are some samples.

• On January 17, 1988, he sent the following urgent dispatch: "With the reinforcement of the tactical group and the 10th Brigade, we are not planning to cross the Cuito River to the east. The defense perimeter east of the river should be reduced by pulling back the 59th and 25th Brigades. . . ."

• Again on February 29: "There has been no answer to two important questions. How many tanks can operate east of the river? How many Angolan tanks in good shape are there to the west?"

• At that point in his reading, Fidel stopped and added some clarifying information: "Since the bulk of troops and equipment were Cuban, President José Eduardo [of Angola] assigned the responsibility of directing the operation to the Cuban military command [i.e., to Castro himself]."

• Then again, on June 7, 1988: "I reiterate the need for peak readiness and protection of troops and the forward use of anti-aircraft weapons. The Pechora regiment from Matala should be moved south as far as possible, preferably at night, to station two groups in Humbe and a group in Cahama. Keep the 85th tactical group there. Tchipa personnel should be kept alert and underground" (*Vindicación*, p. 405).

It was a convincing demonstration of how deeply Castro was involved in the Angolan war. It was *his* war in an almost literal sense, from its beginning when he created it with the dispatch of Cuban troops to Angola in November 1975. Already in 1977, his good friend García Márquez had related how Fidel closely supervised his distant troops from his office in Havana. Now at the session of the State Council, Castro revealed that he dictated the daily battle tactics of a large army seven thousand miles from Cuba and personally produced the final victory of the war. This was a remarkable claim. And while his disclosure was relevant to his main purpose at the trial, one senses that Castro was also moved by a desire to enhance his reputation as a great military leader.

Nevertheless, his immersion in the Angolan war was not necessarily a convincing excuse for his failure to keep track of what was going on in the key Ministry of the Interior. (He had generously given his brother Raúl a clean bill of health in his management of the armed forces.) Fidel is known to have a prodigious capacity for work, attending to even minor details of the nation's business. I recall, for example, the time when he concerned himself with the decision that female nurses should wear trousers instead of skirts. A nurse in skirts leaning over a patient, he suggested with a touch of impish humor, might cause a man lying in a bed behind her to have a heart attack.

Castro went to considerable lengths in attempting to justify the death penalty. He admitted that "different world personalities have addressed us not to apply the death penalty in the case of the accused." He gave no names, but among them was the pope. However, as he saw it, a matter of historic importance was at stake. These are "crucial times for socialism," he declared, "when socialism itself is questioned, when attempts are being made . . . to send it to the trash heap of history." He was asking, in effect, how could anyone take seriously our own effort to purify Cuban socialism if we did not apply the supreme penalty? And for what crime could we apply the death penalty in our statutes if we failed to apply it this time? Fidel did not seem to consider the irony of pleading a case for capital punishment on the basis of purification.

Near the end of his testimony, Castro uncharacteristically seemed to be on the defensive. "Many people [even] in our country," he said, "think that the decision is mine alone." But Castro rejected that assumption. "This is a collective decision," he asserted, although he would favor it in any case because that is his "responsibility." He then explained what he meant by "collective decision." Before the opening of the State Council meeting, he had canvassed every member of the party's highest echelon, the Politburo. They agreed with him unanimously. In the Council of Ministers, only two of its members opposed the death penalty. And in the National Assembly, only one of the 402 deputies present was opposed. If Castro is to be believed, the most surprising revelation was that anybody would openly disagree with him. In any event, it was good public relations; a kind of "democracy" was at work with a tolerance for dissent.

He had reached the end of his testimony. He called for a vote. The State Council unanimously upheld the death penalty. Earlier he had boasted, "Never has history witnessed a cleaner trial" (*Vindicación*, p. 445). It would be closer to the truth to say that never had there been a more elaborate effort to justify a brutal verdict. What purpose was served by executing four obedient and loyal officers? They could well rationalize their drug activities on two counts: (1) subverting American interests, a kind of holy war long promoted by Castro himself; and (2) Cuba's desperate need for convertible currency. They also must have been aware of earlier Cuban cooperation with Colombian drug dealers in return for delivering Cuban weapons to leftist guerrillas. Again, it was a situation where the end justified the means. Meanwhile, the close and scarcely secret relations between the drug-tainted Panamanian ruler, General Manuel Noriega, and Cuban economic and political activities in Panama protected by Noriega helped create a climate of acceptance of drug trafficking by Cubans engaged in resisting the American trade embargo. Finally, as was conceded at the trial, the defendants were scrupulous about keeping the drugs out of circulation within Cuba itself. At the least, there were extenuating circumstances to consider in passing judgment on the accused.

I believe that had Castro not previously denied any Cuban involvement in drug smuggling, there would have been no criminal trial, certainly not one of such spectacular dimensions. Corruption among loyal officers could have been dealt with as before: by censure, demotion, public disgrace, or even brief detention in a not-too-severe work camp. The need for a trial this time was to demonstrate that Fidel Castro had been deceived by his subordinates, that he was utterly opposed to the immorality of drug trafficking, and that the proof of his principled position on this issue would be the severity of the punishment meted out to his close associates who had gone astray.

Paradoxically, the trial did less to vindicate Cuba than to demonstrate in great detail official Cuban complicity in the smuggling of Colombian narcotics to the United States. That Fidel Castro presumably was unaware of the transgression does not relieve him, or his government, of the responsibility of engaging in this criminal activity. Yet that is what the "vindication" purports to do. Nowhere in the trial is there the slightest hint that the exalted leader of the government bore any responsibility for the dereliction of his government. An apology of some sort was in order for Fidel Castro: "I should have been more vigilant. . . . I should have suspected. . . . My distraction with the war in Angola should not have prevented me . . ." and so on. And in this mood it would have been appropriate to temper justice with mercy. But that has never been part of Castro's mind-set. His monumental ego does not admit errors. This time, however, the transgressions were so flagrant that they required vindication on a scale hitherto unknown in the history of the Cuban Revolution. More than any other single event focusing on the nature of Cuban government under Castro, "the cleanest trial in history" served to cast doubt on the political sanity of the Cuban Revolution and on the proposition that the people, the governed, are the ultimate arbiters of political wisdom and justice in Cuba.

10 ★ *Rethinking Fidel Castro*

WOULD THERE HAVE BEEN A Russian Revolution, as we know it, without Lenin? Or a Chinese Revolution without Mao Zedong? These are debatable questions. Without Fidel Castro, would there have been the kind of revolution that completely transformed Cuba and its international relations? The answer in this case is an emphatic no. In recent years, however, it has not been fashionable among scholars to give importance to the role of the individual in the making of history. As a result, the centrality of Castro in the Cuban Revolution is often underestimated.[*]

To be sure, Castro is universally recognized as the creator and leader of the successful insurrection that overthrew

***

[*] See Georgie Anne Geyer, *Guerrilla Prince: The Real Story of the Rise and Fall of Fidel Castro* (Boston, Mass.: Little, Brown, 1991), the most comprehensive and authoritative biography so far.

the Batista dictatorship. But what followed the overthrow is attributed more often than not to a regime or government, or simply to the Cuban nation itself, setting a course in response to internal and external conditions and events. I do not deny that there is a governmental structure in Cuba that maintains law and order, as well as essential domestic and foreign services, a central planning apparatus, and a military establishment. Government makes the bulk of day-to-day administrative decisions; however, I would argue that it is not the Cuban government that has determined policy on major issues, or frequently even on minor ones, but rather the personality of Castro himself.

There is also a Communist party in Cuba, closely modeled on that of the classical ruling party in the former Soviet Union. The difference is that in the case of the Soviet party, an oligarchy known as the Politburo actually determined policy. In Cuba, the corresponding oligarchy is an advisory body. Policy is made by the self-appointed and perpetual first secretary, who is concurrently president of the Republic, chairman of the State Council, chairman of the Council of Ministers, and commander in chief of the armed forces. Following the seizure of power in 1959, the Castro regime ruled by decree. Then, in the mid-1970s, a constitution similar to that of the Soviet Union was belatedly adopted, and the First Congress of the Communist party took place. The Cuban Revolution was thereby said to be institutionalized. What did not occur was a change in the locus of power. On the contrary, the primacy of Fidel Castro was legitimized and thereby enhanced. He remained Cuba's "Jefe Máximo."

The Fourth Congress of the Communist party was held in mid-October 1991. Fidel Castro said it was "the most difficult moment of the Revolution." Responding to the critical economic and social problems resulting from the collapse of trade and aid from the former Communist states of Europe, the most drastic shake-up of membership in the Central Committee and Politburo in twenty-five years took place. More than half of the 225 members of the Central Committee were replaced. The twenty-five-member Politburo lost several of its most distinguished veterans and added fourteen newcomers (*Jornada* [Mexico City] October 13, 16, 1991). The grand shuffle of personalities was supposed to inject youthful energy and new wisdom into the top ranks of the party, but no real change could be expected. That is because Fidel Castro and his brother Raúl, minister of the armed forces and his designated successor, were "reelected" first and second secretary, respectively, of the Central Committee, and they, of course, still dominated the Politburo. Fidel's slogan of the late 1980s, "Socialism or Death," was reaffirmed.

The central fact in this matter is that the Cuban Revolution is preeminently the creation of an extraordinary individual. What forces shaped the young Castro's personality? What has been the source of his power? What has motivated him in the exercise of his power? What moves him in his refusal to share or relinquish his power?

The answer takes us back to 1927, in what was then Oriente Province at the eastern end of the island. A child was born who, through genetic fortune, was endowed with a keen intelligence and robust health. As a youth, he had a commanding stature and handsome features. In addition, he was equipped with an irrepressible ego. Early in life, the child developed symptoms of a personality disorder driving him to rebel against authority and compete ferociously against his schoolmates. Thus, at a very tender age, Fidel threatened his parents and engaged in bitter quarrels with his peers. Even as a child, his perception of what motivated his conduct was "injustice," real or fancied mistreatment by his parents, teachers, and schoolmates.*

At the age of ten or so, he began neglecting his schoolwork in favor of a fascination with military history. By the time of adolescence, his imagination was captured by the deeds of great leaders—José Martí, Bolívar, Napoleon. As a young adult, his earlier perception of personal injustice was transformed into a concern for social justice. Significantly,

* See Carlos Franqui, *Diario de la revolución cubana* (New York: Seaver Books, 1980). Biographical data provided by Franqui are from the tape-recorded conversations between Castro and Franqui, which were the beginning of a projected autobiography that was never completed. The twenty-eight-page transcript takes Fidel through 1948. Additional data supplied by Franqui are from Fidel's correspondence from prison on the Isle of Pines (renamed the Isle of Youth after the Revolution).

he chose Robespierre as a model dispenser of social justice. In a letter written in the mid-fifties, he declared: "Robespierre was an idealist and honorable until his death. . . . It was necessary to be hard, inflexible and severe. . . . A few months of terror were necessary to do away with a terror which had lasted centuries. We need many Robespierres in Cuba."*

A considerable amount of terror has been part of Castro's Cuba for more than thirty years. In 1967, Castro admitted in an interview in *Playboy* (January 1967, p. 74) that there were twenty thousand "counter-revolutionary criminals" in Cuban prisons. Many were serving twenty-five-year terms. In 1986, two books by former long-term prisoners spelled out in convincing detail the brutal mistreatment of political prisoners in Castro's gulag: *Against All Hope* by Armando Valladares and *Twenty Years and Forty Days: Life in a Cuban Prison* by Jorge Valls. According to the reputable Americas Watch Committee, "Over time . . . evidence accumulated that Cuba held more political prisoners as a percentage of population than any other country in the world. . . . Only South Africa, Indonesia, and possibly the People's Republic of China came close. Neither the Soviet Union nor any other country in the Soviet bloc approached Cuba's distressing record."**

* Cited by Heberto Padilla, *Self-Portrait of the Other: A Memoir* (New York: Farrar, Straus and Giroux, 1990), 238.
** Jorge Valls, *Twenty Years and Forty Days: Life in a Cuban Prison,* an Americas Watch Report (New York: Americas Watch, 1986), iii.

By the time Castro launched his insurrection, he already displayed symptoms of megalomania. He was convinced that he was engaged in a historic mission. Like Moses or José Martí he would lead his people out of bondage. Once in power, he felt impelled to liberate the oppressed peoples of Latin America. And in middle age, he sent Cuban armies to support revolution in Africa. There is an additional component of Castro's personality that helps explain his amazing success as a leader. It is his charisma, a mysterious but real, almost hypnotic power, which attracted the intense, unquestioning loyalty of his earliest followers and then captivated the great mass of the Cuban people. Combining his charisma with a rare oratorical virtuosity, Castro could hold a million people spellbound for hours at a time. He had surpassed anybody in previous Cuban history as the anointed leader of the Cuban people. To be effective, the charismatic leader must also have convincing credentials, and in this too Fidel Castro was well equipped. He was the warrior-hero who risked his life in an apparently hopeless struggle to overthrow tyranny and, by a miracle, managed to survive. After undergoing incredible hardships, he emerged as the supreme military and political leader of a victorious insurrection. He was the right man in the right place at the right time and with the right message.

Castro, of course, was not raised in a vacuum. He was brought up in a country that had produced José Martí, a revered intellectual giant and martyred freedom fighter; a country that had undergone a great political and social upheaval during his childhood; a country in which a Communist party had briefly flourished; a country dominated by a foreign power. Traditions of nationalism and of striving for political and social reform molded a significant part of Cuban culture that Castro's generation had absorbed. And there was, in addition, the Hispanic precedent of *caudillismo* (strongman leadership), which was to serve Castro in his exercise of power.

The collapse of constitutional government in 1952 ignited violent resistance, particularly among Cuban youth. The aims of the resistance, including those voiced by the young Castro, were typically Cuban: a restoration of constitutional government; elimination of corruption; implementation of economic and social reforms; and, as a minor theme, a more equitable relationship with the United States. Except for a minuscule and largely discredited Communist party (at the time calling itself the Popular Socialist party), conspicuously absent from any dissident program at the time was anything remotely resembling a Marxist-Leninist orientation or the slightest reference to the Soviet system as a model for Cuba. In other words, there was nothing to suggest that objective or subjective conditions existed that could lead to transforming Cuba almost overnight into a Marxist-Leninist state allied with the Soviet Union.

That this historically unprecedented phenomenon occurred can be attributed only to Fidel Castro. At what particular time he conceived the option of fundamentally restructuring Cuban society and Cuba's foreign relations is a matter of speculation. According to his claim in a speech on July 26, 1988, he had been "thinking about the Revolution even before March 10, 1952 [the date of Batista's coup]. . . . Starting out from the principles of socialism, of Marxism-Leninism . . . we said: There are objective conditions in Cuba for a revolution, what's missing are subjective conditions. . . . We were thinking of a profound revolution that sooner or later had to become a socialist revolution" (*Granma Weekly Review*, August 7, 1988). In that case, he cunningly kept it a secret, making deceptive statements for many years. Thus, in a press conference in New York on April 23, 1959, some three months after taking power, he said, "We want to establish in Cuba a true democracy without any trace of Fascism, Peronism, or Communism. We are against any kind of totalitarianism."* Yet we know that early on, Castro was attracted to what he called "utopian socialism."*** Later, as a university student, he did some reading of Marx, Engels, and Lenin and became acquainted with a few Communist students. However, he never joined the party or any of its affiliated organizations and wisely kept them at arm's length.

In Mexico, while preparing for his return to Cuba, he

---

* Herbert L. Matthews, *Fidel Castro* (New York: Simon and Schuster, 1969), 161.
** Franqui, 17.

read Stalin—apparently after Khrushchev's revelations of Stalin's crimes. Nevertheless, his attitude toward the Soviet despot was positive, consistent with his admiration of Robespierre.* While denying any leaning toward communism during and for two years after his insurrection, at no time did he establish the credentials of an anti-Communist or condemn the Soviet Union. One may conclude that even before taking power, he was intellectually and emotionally prepared for the socialist or Communist revolution he was to launch early in the sixties.

Another significant aspect of his early political orientation was his deep-seated hostility toward the United States. Later, that became a considerable asset in drawing support from Latin American radical nationalists. Gabriel García Márquez was quoted in 1990 as saying that "Castro is the necessary thorn in the lion's paw." If it were not for this visionary leader's defiance of the empire, "the United States would be into Latin America all the way to Patagonia."** On June 5, 1958, half a year before toppling the Batista regime, he wrote in confidence to his intimate companion Celia Sánchez: "When this war is over, a much longer and bigger war will begin for me: the war which I will make

---

* Franqui, 153. In Mexico, Franqui found Fidel and Che studying Stalin's *Fundamentos del Leninismo* (Foundations of Leninism). According to Franqui, Fidel expressed "una opinión lapidaria," i.e., bedrock approval, of Stalin's iron-fisted rule of the USSR.
** Anthony Day and Marjorie Miller, "Gabo Talks," *Los Angeles Times Magazine,* Sept. 2, 1990.

against [the Americans]. I realize this will be my true destiny."* Was he already contemplating a strategy of attracting the support of the Soviet Union to assure the fulfillment of his "true destiny"? In a speech carried in the April 3, 1959, issue of Havana's *El Mundo,* he declared, "This revolution will take its place as one of the greatest political events in history." At the time, his boast appeared to be the product of an overheated imagination.

The publication at the end of 1988 of the memoirs of Alexandr Alexeev, who had been the first Soviet ambassador to Cuba, has shed new light on the chronology of Castro's decision to move Cuba toward socialism and an alliance with the Soviet Union. Alexeev reveals that he first met Che Guevara in Havana on October 12, 1959. According to Alexeev, Che told him that "in his personal opinion, in order to win freedom and independence for Cuba there was no other path except the construction of a socialist society and the establishment of friendly relations with the countries of the socialist commonwealth." Three days later, Alexeev met with Fidel Castro. Although Castro was not as explicit as Che, his remarks indicated a similar point of view. He told Alexeev that "Cuban public opinion was still subject to the influence of anti-Soviet and anti-Communist propaganda and as yet was not ready to reestablish diplomatic relations with the USSR." To remedy the situation,

---

* Cited by Jorge Domínguez, *To Make a World Safe for Revolution: Cuban Foreign Policy* (Cambridge: Harvard Univ. Press, 1989), 30.

Castro proposed that "a Soviet trade exhibit, which at the time was on display in Mexico, be put on display in Havana."*

Thus, it was not the Soviets but Castro who initiated the project. The exhibition opened in Havana in February 1960, with the presence of Anastas Mikoyan, the number two man in the ruling Soviet hierarchy. According to Alexeev, he had "the warmest . . . relations with Fidel. . . . It was then that the Cubans actually began to believe that the USSR would selflessly assist Cuba."** One could also add that it marked the beginnings of what would turn out to be one of the great ironies of our times, when the Soviet Union abandoned Cuba some thirty years later and then vanished from the international scene altogether.

I believe that Castro had set his course to the extreme left no later than mid-October 1959. His determination of that direction helps explain the urgency and ferocity with which he turned against the anti-Communist Huber Matos, an able and loyal *comandante* in the Sierra. In the trumped-up trial, Castro personally charged him with treason and dictated a sentence of twenty years. It also accounts for Cas-

* Alexandr Alexeev, "The Caribbean Crisis: As It Really Was," *Ekho Planyeti* (Moscow), no. 33 (Nov. 1988): 26–27. Years later, Castro was more explicit: "To be a free and independent country . . . we had to sweep away the capitalist system" (speech on July 26, 1990, *Granma Weekly Review,* Aug. 5, 1990). I am grateful to James G. Blight for bringing the Alexeev article to my attention. Alexeev, incidentally, fully corroborates Carlos Franqui's insightful discussion of Mikoyan's visit. See Franqui, *Diario,* 128–29.
** Alexeev, 26, 27.

tro's seemingly irrational refusal soon after taking power to consider any proposal that could lead to an amicable settlement of his quarrel with the United States. As Heberto Padilla, Cuba's preeminent poet in exile, laments, "It was the start of the fatal process which . . . turns the revolutionary party into a bureaucratic caste and its leader into a Caesar."*

Castro's strategy of using the cold war to enlist the support of the Soviet Union in order to move Cuba out of the orbit of the United States bears the stamp of genius and of his propensity to take great risks. The implementation of his strategy was another extraordinary feat of timing, both within Cuba and on the international scene. He bolstered his stature of hero and redeemer by providing the Cuban masses overnight with substantial economic and social benefits, paid for by state funds accumulated under capitalism and, at the same time, arousing their sense of nationalism. Step by step he manipulated a sometimes reluctant Kremlin to assume the role of his protector. When he finally declared at the beginning of December 1961 that he was a "Marxist-Leninist" and would remain one for the rest of his life, he had successfully locked Cuba into a new system of domestic and international relations.

It was an incredible tour de force. Less than three years had passed since he took power in a country where, at the time, in the words of the late President Osvaldo Dorticós, "a large part of our population—let us mention this with com-

* Padilla, 181, 182.

plete frankness—even a large part of our workers were frightened by the very word socialism."*

Castro's failures, like his triumphs, bear the imprint of his monumental ego, his reckless self-confidence and, most important, his unchallenged authority. Consider, as an example, his disastrous project to produce a ten-million-ton sugar harvest in 1970, Castro's "sugar atomic bomb." It was a personal decision made without paying any attention to his sugar experts, who knew it could not be done. The wild project was motivated by a quixotic dream of gaining control of the world sugar market. That he survived the ensuing economic catastrophe was another tribute to his charismatic grip on the Cuban people.

Castro's survival has been due, in large part, to his great skill in fostering Cuban nationalism, that is to say, anti-Americanism. The history of prerevolutionary Cuba supported him, and U.S. hostility since the early sixties reinforced the fear of Yankee imperialism. Throughout the years, Castro and his public relations experts have made sure that Cubans did not forget the humiliations of the Platt Amendment, the U.S. naval base at Guantánamo Bay, or the more recent Bay of Pigs invasion. In addition, the United States has been blamed for the need to maintain a powerful military establishment, and the trade embargo has been cited over and over as the reason for economic failures.

At the same time, nationalism has served another

* *Cuba Socialista,* no. 1 (Sept. 1961): 28.

important purpose. By combining nationalism and socialism, Castro legitimized socialism. Year after year Castro has
repeated in his speeches to the Cuban people that socialism,
or communism and Marxism-Leninism, was not imposed
from the outside. Thus, Castro managed to "cubanize"
socialism, much as Mao Zedong "sinotized" Marxism. Castro and Mao stand in contrast to the tyrants of the erstwhile
Soviet bloc in Eastern Europe, who had been imposed by
Moscow. For Castro, only through socialism can Cuba
maintain its independence—"socialismo o muerte." Otherwise, it would once again become a mere appendage of the
American empire and a happy hunting ground for thousands of returning Cuban exiles from Miami. Castro's argument has an effective appeal for some older Cubans who
remember prerevolutionary Cuba but is less effective among
younger Cubans, who associate steadily declining standards
of living and the less and less tolerable regimentation of
their personal lives with the socialism they have known
under Castro.

DURING MY VISIT to Havana at the close of 1989, I noted
that Cuba's economic crisis was the worst the country had
experienced since Castro came to power. Nevertheless, it
was apparent that he remained firmly in control. The magic
of his charisma, what García Márquez called "his terrible
power to seduce his listeners,"* had not diminished. I felt at

* Cited by Robert McCrum, *Manchester Guardian Weekly*, March 17, 1991, 22.

the time that if a plebiscite were held in Cuba, like the one ending General Pinochet's rule in Chile, Castro's leadership would in fact be confirmed. It seemed to me that economic conditions would have to get much worse before Castro's survival would be threatened. Yet two years later they did get much worse. His survival as Cuba's leader has now come very much into question.

Recent visitors report that the scarcity of raw materials, particularly petroleum, formerly supplied by the Soviet Union and East European satellites, has forced the shut down of factories and the abandonment of building projects. It appears, for example, that the uncompleted nuclear energy plant at Juraguá, in south central Cuba, under construction since 1985 with the help of some two hundred Soviet technicians, will remain unfinished. That may be a blessing in disguise, given that the safety of a Soviet-designed plant employing inexperienced Cubans would be questionable at best. Its proximity to Florida, the direction of the prevailing winds, and its location in a coastal area frequently swept by hurricanes and tidal waves have been matters of concern in the United States for some time.

Transportation services have been drastically reduced, and so has the use of electrical appliances, even television. Serious shortages of medical supplies in hospitals and pharmacies are common. One reporter (*Los Angeles Times*, November 17, 1991) discovered that meat was available to most residents of Havana a total of just four days in the first ten months of 1991. And availability of consumer goods is likely to get worse, not better. Thousands of urban Cubans have been sent on rotation to the countryside, where inexperience and a lack of agricultural machinery, sufficient fertilizer of any kind, and insect control result in low yields of food crops. At the same time, heroic efforts are required to maintain normal production in the all-important sugar industry. Meanwhile, visible political discontent and attempts at illegal emigration have been rising.

In a major speech on December 27, 1991 (*Granma Weekly Review*, December 31, 1991), Castro himself summed up Cuba's economic predicament by explaining that while the value of annual imports from the Soviet Union usually amounted to $5 billion, "this year the figure, up to this moment, is one billion, 673 million. Can you imagine a more drastic reduction? . . . Add to this the disappearance of trade with the socialist camp, not counting the Soviet Union, beginning in 1990." And now, to make matters worse, the Soviet Union has actually disappeared. "It does not exist!" He particularly stressed the critical situation of fuel imports, revealing that 530,000 single-gear, hard-to-pump Chinese bicycles were in use on the streets of Havana. Anticipating that 1992 could be an even more difficult year, he nevertheless promised that "we will continue to defend the Revolution, to defend socialism."

Castro's expectation about the decline of the Cuban economy was later confirmed. As reported in the *Economist*

(April 24, 1993), an "unusually frank study published in Havana by the Centre of American Studies, a Communist Party think-tank, reckons that the island cannot generate even 40% of the income needed to buy essential consumer goods abroad. . . . [In addition] a leaked Cuban government report . . . discloses that Cuba's total reserves in hard currency and precious metals fell from $102m in 1991 to $12m in 1992. Of 515 items defined as essential for domestic production, 226 were not available last year. Of the others, availability wavered between 5% and 26% in the 1980's, when Soviet aid still flowed."

For a time, Castro could hope that the old guard hard-liners in Moscow, sympathetic to maintaining the traditional Soviet-Cuban alliance, would regain control of the Kremlin. This hope vanished with the failed Moscow coup in August 1991, followed by the dissolution of the Soviet Communist party to which Cuba's Communist party could look for fraternal support. Finally, at the very end of 1991, the Soviet Union itself disappeared, with no indication that the remaining hard-pressed independent states had either the interest or the economic capacity to come to Cuba's rescue. Since then, political uncertainties in Moscow in early 1992 and after may have revived a glimmer of hope in Havana. Some fifteen thousand pro-Communists demonstrated in Moscow on February 9, shouting "Yeltsin the Judas," and waving pictures of Lenin, Stalin and Castro" (*New York Times*, February 10, 1992).

As Castro's economy crumbles and the Soviet Union dissolves—leaving Cuba without its economic and military protector—Cuba's isolation grows increasingly untenable in a world that has largely rejected communism, including the Cuban model. The exceptions are Vietnam (showing a certain amount of flexibility), North Korea, and China in its political, but not economic, structure. Vietnam and North Korea are in deep economic depression, and China's capacity to solve Cuba's problems is negligible. Nelson Mandela's and the South African Communist party's undiminished infatuation with the Cuban Revolution can be of only small comfort to Castro. The Cuban role in the Third World, excepting Latin America, has been reduced to the vanishing point.

Socialist Cuba's many years of isolation from the rest of Latin America have ended. Nearly all countries now maintain diplomatic and commercial relations. The reasons can be summed up as follows: (1) With the failure of Marxism in Nicaragua and a peace settlement in El Salvador, Cuban support for leftist insurgencies there and in other countries has dried up; (2) in Latin America, renewing relations with Cuba has become a symbol of opposition to past and possible future violations of sovereignty by the United States; and (3) as Cuban isolation in the rest of the world has grown, Castro has increasingly invoked common language and history to promote the acceptance of Cuba in the fraternity of Latin American nations.

Castro's presence at the First Ibero-American Summit, held in Guadalajara, Mexico, in mid-July 1991, was hailed by Havana propaganda as a great moral and political triumph for the Cuban Revolution. It was something less than that, although still noteworthy. The meeting was attended by twenty-one heads of state from Latin American countries, as well as from Spain and Portugal. Castro was invited by President Carlos Salinas de Gortari of Mexico and not by a consensus of summit participants. Mexico is the only Latin American country that never broke relations with Cuba, a concession to pressures from the Mexican anti-imperialist left.

In his speech, Castro appealed for Latin American investment and increased trade. With respect to "joint ventures," he offered "preferential treatment for our Latin American partners. . . including Latin American capital contributions greater than 50 per cent." Concerning trade, he suggested "new means of compensated bartering" (*Granma International*, August 4, 1992). If he intended to reveal a new pragmatism, he was unconvincing. He made no concessions with respect to moderating his dictatorship and denounced the United States with his usual vigor: "We [Latin Americans] have been divided, attacked, cut in pieces, occupied, kept underdeveloped, plundered." Practically all the other countries at the summit were committed to democratic and capitalist development. They were eager to improve economic and political relations with the United

States. Thus, in addition to the unacceptable business risks, they could scarcely find it prudent to accept Castro's overtures.

In any event, there was no public response to his appeal. Privately, President Felipe González Márquez of Spain poked fun at the bearded Cuban leader for wearing his military uniform at the meeting, the only leader not in civilian clothes. (Castro has not been seen in civilian dress since late November 1956, when he sailed from Mexico to begin his insurrection.) Portuguese President Mario Soares (like President González, a moderate socialist) told journalists that Castro was "a dinosaur, respectable only because he is prehistoric" (*Globe and Mail* [Toronto], July 27, 1991). As Mark A. Uhlig of the *New York Times* (July 28, 1991) concluded, "The participating heads of state invariably looked straight past Mr. Castro's national predicament, focusing instead on the hardheaded business of building a new global negotiating block that could unite the markets and policies of their nations. . . . In the conflict of Latin American politics that he helped provoke and define, it appeared that Mr. Castro would even be denied the honor of a final losing battle."

The First Ibero-American Summit could have been a strategic opportunity for Castro to offer an initial indication of Cuban reform, or at least some hint of a new ideological, political, and economic pragmatism. It might have improved the reception of his plea for joint ventures, which was unattractive, among other reasons, as long as it involved partnership with a repressive Marxist-Leninist regime that was clearly destined to die. An unspoken assumption at the summit was that only a miracle, such as a major shift in American policy, could prolong the life of socialism in Cuba, but that such a shift was most unlikely to occur as long as Castro remained in power. Castro, on the other hand, expected no miracle. The signal he appeared to send from Guadalajara in July 1991 was that if his ship was destined to sink, he intended to go down with it.

Castro sent a similar signal from the United Nations in mid-December 1991. Cuba was one of the few states that voted against revoking the 1975 resolution equating Zionism with racism, which Cuba had originally supported. In so doing, Cuba found itself aligned with Iraq, Libya, North Korea, Syria, Vietnam, and a few other unreconstructed centers of autocracy and bigotry. Deciding not to give Zionism a clean bill of health, Cuba could have abstained, as Ethiopia did, or might have been absent at voting time, as in the case of China. But for Castro there was no compromise with imperialism on this issue, indeed suggesting no compromise on any other.

Personally, Castro has never been anti-Semitic. At one time he claimed to be descended from Sephardic Jews,* who were victims of the Spanish Inquisition in the fifteenth

---

* Halperin, *Taming of Fidel Castro,* 241. See also chapters 29, 30, and 31 on Castro and the Jews (236–55).

century and among whom *Castro* was a common name. Castro refused to follow the lead of the Soviet Union in breaking relations with Israel after the Arab-Israeli war of 1967. When he did break relations in 1973, it was purely an opportunistic decision to appease the Arab states. It paid off because he gained their support in being elected leader of the Nonaligned Movement in 1979. At the end of 1991, he was still in no mood for reconciliation with Israel and the Jewish Diaspora. Instead, he preferred a stubborn affirmation of cold war doctrine, a foreign policy decision that matched the rigidity of domestic policy and a defiance of pragmatic rationality.

Castro is intelligent and well informed. He must realize that the odds are overwhelmingly against him. In the past, he has occasionally showed surprising flexibility. For example, in 1964, he offered to abandon Cuban export of revolution to Latin America in return for normalization of relations with the United States but was rebuffed by Washington. Then again, in 1970, he acknowledged defeat of his ultraleftist deviations from Soviet-style Marxism-Leninism and accepted the Stalinist model in return for the Kremlin's rescue of Cuba's bankrupt economy. It is significant that in both cases his flexibility posed no threat to his personal power. However, in the post-cold war crisis, he apparently fears that any modification of Cuba's command economy or liberalization of control of the state by the Cuban Communist party would initially weaken him and eventually eliminate his monopoly of power. That glasnost and perestroika, after some five years, led to the dissolution of the Communist party of the Soviet Union and then the dismantlement of the Soviet state itself undoubtedly reinforced his antipathy to "reform."

This brings us back to the personality disorder that Castro displayed as a child and throughout the rest of his life. He has had an uncontrollable compulsion to lead and to dominate—the results of an innate conviction of his superiority and of his destiny to make history. Until the collapse of communism in most of the world, his mission was to liberate the oppressed masses of the Third World. Now with equal pride, he has taken on another historic role: the last Communist who refuses to surrender to imperialism. Watching him on TV in my hotel room in 1989, he looked older by all of the quarter century that had passed since I had last seen him. He was sixty-two years old. The trim, handsome lines of his face had become flabby. His black beard had turned nearly entirely gray, and his formerly flat abdomen was now a rounded potbelly. On the other hand, his mind was as nimble as ever, projecting sincerity while concealing cunning calculations. The modulation of his high-pitched voice, his piercing black eyes, the prominent eyebrows he raised or lowered to make a point, and the wild flinging of his arms were all still there. Castro remained the supreme virtuoso of political oratory.

It now seems highly improbable that the Cuban Revolu-

still here 20 yrs later!

tion and its creator, Fidel Castro, can survive. Although one cannot predict how much longer the regime will last, the end will come sooner rather than later. It is to be expected that the transition to a multiparty and private enterprise system will be difficult in Cuba as in all the former Communist party states, though with variations in some particulars. For example, Cuba is culturally a homogeneous society and, thus, has no basis for ethnic conflict. On the other hand, the removal of Fidel Castro and his brother from power, likely a prerequisite for transition, will create a power vacuum that did not exist in Europe, with the possible exception of Ceauşescu's Romania. This difference could easily lead to violence, as ambitious and hitherto frustrated generals with combat experience in Angola and Ethiopia compete to fill the vacuum. Cuba, moreover, is saturated with weapons and full of men and women who know how to use them. All in all, it is unlikely that the transition will be peaceful.

As a result, the future of Cuba could pose some unpleasant problems for the United States. On the one hand, one could anticipate a mass exodus of Cubans seeking safety or reunion with relatives in the United States, adding strains on an already overburdened immigration and welfare system. Moving in the other direction a significant number of long-exiled Cubans, many of whom are now American citizens, might attempt to return home, recover their expropriated properties, and develop investment opportunities.

These elements would add to the confusion and conflicts during the transition period. Under these circumstances, there might well be pressures within both the United States and Cuba for American military intervention to restore law and order. There would, of course, be resistance in the United States to such a policy as well as strong opposition in Latin America. Privately, the Presidents of Mexico, Venezuela, and Colombia tried to impress on Castro and others at the Guadalajara Summit the need for a peaceful transition in Cuba to avoid the possibility of American intervention, which could provoke serious domestic problems in their respective countries.

Nevertheless, both the American concern over Cuba's strategic location ninety miles south of Florida and the abiding U.S. eagerness for commercial opportunities in Cuba have deep historic roots. As early as 1803, soon after the Louisiana Purchase, Thomas Jefferson expressed a strong interest in acquiring the island, and he continued to promote the idea after leaving the presidency in 1809. More recently, the Soviet attempt to place nuclear missiles in Cuba, along with forty-three thousand Soviet troops to defend them, served as a reminder that U.S. interests are not removed from the fate of the island.

I LEFT CUBA on December 5, 1989, with a heavy heart. During our extended stay in Cuba in the 1960s, Edith and

I had become fond of the Cuban people and their beautiful island. The physical deterioration of Havana, the increased deprivations of the inhabitants, and the likelihood of an even bleaker future for them depressed me greatly. Cuba is a vivid green all year long, with an abundance of bright flowers blooming in all seasons. The sun shines three hundred days a year. It has magnificent, easily accessible beaches. Because of the trade winds, its tropical climate is mild, ideal for human habitation. There is no need for indoor heating or winter clothing, an advantage that Cuban socialism has had over its former benefactors in Eastern Europe. In my experience, the Cuban people are as congenial as their natural environment. They display a friendly warmth and seem naturally convivial. Cubans are a physically attractive people, proud in bearing, open in gesture. I found them singularly lacking in ethnic or religious bigotry. (I encountered no slur term for Jew in Cuba, which may be a unique phenomenon in the Christian world. Jews in Cuba are usually called *Polacos*, because most came from Poland after the First World War, but there is nothing derogatory in the term.) Even those most affected by Castro's anti-American propaganda seemed always to distinguish between the American government and individual Americans. Never once did Edith and I encounter hostility because of our nationality. We led a full social life, contrary to our experience in Moscow, where we were in near isolation from the Russian people. I fondly remember participating in the weekly chamber music sessions at our home with Cuban and foreign musicians from the National Symphony Orchestra.

To be sure, we had encountered ominous symptoms of the dark side of socialism, especially in the later sixties. Critical discourse, except among trusted friends and relatives, had to be muted. We knew the prisons were filling up. It was like a black shadow partially obscuring the sun. The recurrent shortages of consumer goods were annoying. I recall how difficult it was to get enough gasoline for a friend to drive me to the airport when I left Cuba in the spring of 1968.

Nevertheless, it is fair to say that in the sixties most Cubans still had hope. They remembered the evil days under Batista. Despite the difficulties, probably a large majority of Cubans felt that the Revolution had improved the quality of life. Castro was erratic and could be cruel, but few doubted his dedication to the common welfare. And Cubans had national pride in their defiance of the mighty Yankees, a feat that no other Latin American country had achieved. At the same time, confidence grew in the continuing economic and military support of the powerful Soviet Union. No one suspected the future collapse of the great benefactor or dreamed of Castro's irrationality when confronted with that catastrophe.

At the close of 1989, in contrast, I found the popular

mood one of deep discouragement, perhaps born of suppressed anger after decades of seemingly unending and increasing austerity. I could see the toll being paid in the weary and cheerless faces I passed on the street. Cuba's whole body language had changed. *Habaneros* seemed to plod along glumly, contrasting with my memories of their earlier brisk walk and animated conversation. I wondered how they managed to carry on. Apparently, life in some respects was still tolerable. The weather was still warm and beautiful beaches were still close by. Lovers, as always, embraced along the Malecón, the embankment bordering the Gulf of Mexico. Via television and American and Western European movies, Cubans could vicariously enjoy the pleasures of affluent society. There was plenty of first-rate baseball, to which Cubans are passionately addicted, and admission was free. The great and welcome distraction of 1991 was the Pan American Games, held in Havana for the first time.

Thus, Cuba has its version of bread and circuses, a formula that worked in ancient Rome. But with diminishing rations of bread, the formula is not doing well. Young Cubans especially are skeptical. More than half the population is too young to remember the Batista dictatorship. For this half, only the present and future matter. It was not so long ago when Castro promised a bright future. Now his favorite slogan is "Socialism or Death." I cannot imagine any young Cuban, or even many older Cubans, prepared to die for socialism. Yet, I fear that some—perhaps many—will die in the task of liberating Cuba from socialism.

That was the saddest thought of all as I departed from Cuba, probably never to return.

Bibliography

WORKS CITED

Alexeev, Alexandr. "The Caribbean Crisis: As It Really Was." *Ekho Planyeti* (Moscow), no. 33 (Nov. 1988): 26–27.

Bayer, R. and C. Healton. "Controlling AIDS in Cuba: The Logic of Quarantine." *New England Journal of Medicine* 15 (1989): 1022–24.

Day, Anthony and Marjorie Miller. "Gabo Talks." *Los Angeles Times Magazine,* Sept. 2, 1990.

Domínguez, Jorge I. *To Make a World Safe for Revolution: Cuban Foreign Policy.* Cambridge, Mass.: Harvard Univ. Press, 1989.

Domínguez, Jorge I. and Rafael Hernández, eds. *U.S.-Cuban Relations in the 1990s.* Boulder, Colo.: Westview Press, 1989.

Fernández, Marcelo. *Cuba y la economía azucarera mundial.* Havana, 1989.

Franqui, Carlos. *Diario de la revolución cubana.* New York: Seaver Books, 1980.

Geyer, Georgie Anne. *Guerrilla Prince: The Real Story of the Rise and Fall of Fidel Castro.* Boston: Little, Brown, 1991.

Halperin, Maurice. *The Rise and Decline of Fidel Castro: An Essay in Contemporary History.* Berkeley: Univ. of California Press,

1972.

_____. *The Taming of Fidel Castro.* Berkeley: Univ. of California Press, 1981.

James, Daniel. *Che Guevara: A Biography.* Chelsea, Mich.: Scarborough House, 1970.

Matthews, Herbert L. *Fidel Castro.* New York: Simon and Schuster, 1969.

Mesa-Lago, Carmelo. "Countdown in Cuba?" *Hemisfile,* March 1990, 7.

O'Connor, James. "On Cuban Political Economy." *Political Science Quarterly* 19 (1964): 233–47.

Padilla, Heberto. *Self-Portrait of the Other: A Memoir.* New York: Farrar, Straus and Giroux, 1990.

United Nations Statistical Yearbook. New York: United Nations, 1960.

Valls, Jorge. *Twenty Years and Forty Days: Life in a Cuban Prison,* an Americas Watch Report. New York: Americas Watch, 1986.

NEWS JOURNALS

Boston Globe
Chicago Tribune
Cuba Socialista
Economist (London)
El País (Madrid)
Excelsior (Mexico City)
Foreign Affairs
Globe and Mail (Toronto)
Granma (Havana)
Granma International (Havana)
Granma Weekly Review (Havana)
Latin American Weekly Report

Le Monde
Los Angeles Times
Manchester Guardian Weekly
Nation
New Republic
New York Times
Sun (Vancouver, B.C.)
Washington Post

FURTHER READING

Blight, James G. and David Welsh. *On the Brink: Americans and Soviets Reexamine the Cuban Missile Crisis.* New York: Hill and Wang, 1989.

Draper, Theodore. *Castroism: Theory and Practice.* New York: Frederick A. Praeger, 1965.

Dumont, René. *Is Cuba Socialist?* Translated by Stanley Hochman. London: André Deutsch, 1974.

Franqui, Carlos. *Family Portrait with Fidel: A Memoir.* Translated by Alfred MacAdam. New York: Random House, 1984.

González, Edward and David Ronfeldt. *Castro, Cuba and the World.* Santa Monica, Calif.: Rand, 1986.

Higgins, Trumbull. *The Perfect Failure: Kennedy, Eisenhower and the CIA at the Bay of Pigs.* New York: W. W. Norton, 1987.

Horowitz, Irving Louis, ed. *Cuban Communism.* 7th ed. New Brunswick, N.J.: Transaction Publishers, 1989.

Karol, K. S. *Guerrillas in Power: The Course of the Cuban Revolution.* Translated by Arnold Pomerans. New York: Hill and Wang, 1970.

Lockwood, Lee. *Castro's Cuba, Cuba's Fidel: An American Journalist's*

Inside Look at Today's Cuba in Text and Picture. New York: Macmillan, 1967.

Mesa-Lago, Carmelo. *The Economy of Socialist Cuba: A Two Decade Appraisal.* Albuquerque: Univ. of New Mexico Press, 1981.

Montaner, Carlos Alberto. *Cuba, Castro and the Caribbean: The Cuban Revolution and the Crisis in Western Conscience.* Translated by Nelson Duran. New Brunswick, N.J.: Transaction Publishers, 1985.

Oppenheimer, Andrés. *Castro's Final Hour.* New York: Simon and Schuster, 1992.

Quirk, Robert E. *Fidel Castro.* New York: W. W, Norton, 1993.

Radosh, Ronald, ed. *The New Cuba: Paradoxes and Potentials.* New York: William Morrow, 1976.

Smith, Wayne. *The Closest of Enemies: A Personal and Diplomatic Account of U.S.-Cuban Relations Since 1957.* New York: W. W. Norton, 1987.

Szulc, Tad. *Fidel: A Critical Portrait.* New York: William Morrow, 1986.

Thomas, Hugh. *Cuba: The Pursuit of Freedom.* New York: Harper and Row, 1971.

Timerman, Jacobo. *Cuba: A Journey.* New York: Alfred A. Knopf, 1991.

Valladares, Armando. *Against All Hope: The Prison Memoirs of Armando Vallardes.* Translated by Andrew Hurley. New York: Alfred A. Knopf, 1986.

Index

Abrantes, José, 142
Agriculture. *See* Sugar
AIDS, 132–36, 137; and *sidatoria,* 132
Alexeev, Alexander, 172, 173
Americas Watch Committee, 167
Angola, 42, 65, 102, 108–20, 140, 144, 146, 148, 152, 153, 154, 186; as Cuban colony, 110; and Cold War, 118; Cuba-Angola compared with U.S.-Vietnam, 110–11; Cuban popular support for, 111–12

Bagasse, 103, 104
Bankhead, Tallulah, 2
Bassols, Narciso, 11
Bay of Pigs, 20, 112, 175
Beals, Carleton, 2
Ben Bella, Mohammed Ahmed, 114
Boletín Especial (public health in Holguín). *See* Health-care system
Bolívar, Simón, 166
Borah, Woodrow   8
Boston University, 10
Bread, Cuban, 31–32
Brigades (*see also* Contingents), 62
Bulgaria, 31, 52, 63n, 75, 76, 103

Castro: admiration of Robespierre, 167, 169, of Stalin, 170; and betrayal 155; charisma, 168; choice of socialist revolution, 170; credibility and honor undermined, 140–41; and "Cubanization" of socialism, 176; and drug trafficking, 156–59; on Eastern bloc exports, 75–76; on failure of the sugar industry, 105; on Havana's deterioration, 40–41; and Israel, 184; as leader of Nonaligned

Movement, 184; personal conduct of Angolan war, 156–58; personal hostility toward United States, 171–72; personality disorder, 155, 166, 168, 175, 185; *Playboy* interview, 167; portrait of in 1989, 185; promotion of Cuban nationalism, 175; and propaganda machine, 40; roles in Ochoa trial, 144; speeches: (4/3/59), 172; (9/60), 112; (5/2/71), 136; (12/2/86), 137; (1/11/87), 77; (7/26/88), 168; (11/7/89), 39–43; (7/26/90), 173n; (7/91), 181; (12/27/91), 178; use of Cold War, 174
Castro, Raúl, 148, 149, 150, 154, 159, 165
China, People's Republic of, 58, 79, 116, 118, 167, 180, 183; and foreign relations with Cuba, 51, 98; and rice imports from Cuba, 50
Communist Party of Cuba, 86, 91, 93, 144, 151, 164, 169; Castro's control of, 86, 156, 184; First Congress of, 73, 87, 164; Third Congress of, 105; Fourth Congress of, 165; and health-care system, 121, 125; and Soviet party, 164, 179
Contingents (*see also* Brigades), 40, 62, 63

De la Guardia, Antonio, 145–49
Dentistry, 21
Department MC, 147–48
Deutsch, Karl, 8
Dollar, dependency on, 14, 27, 154
Domínguez, Jorge, 95, 172

RETURN TO HAVANA

was composed electronically in 12 on 16 Adobe Garamond
(the first typeface specifically designed for Postscript,
the digital language that is used for computer types),
with display type in Futura;
printed on 60-pound, acid-free Phoenix Smooth Recycled Natural paper,
with 80-pound Multicolor endsheets,
Smyth-sewn and bound over 88-point binder's boards
in Arrestox B cloth
by Braun-Brumfield, Inc.;
with dust jackets printed in 4 colors
by Vanderbilt University Printing Services.
Both book and jacket design are the work of Gary Gore,
using Quark Express on a Macintosh computer.
Published by Vanderbilt University Press,
Nashville, Tennessee 37235.

P, 95-98
great summary